Discarded Lives

Myrna Whitman Conrad

xulon
PRESS

Discarded Lives
by Myrna Whitman Conrad

Printed in the United States of America

ISBN 978-1-60266-488-3

www.xulonpress.com

Prologue

Angela floated buoyantly in the warm, secure blanket of fluid that surrounded her tiny, little body; freely moving in her mother's womb, yet ever connected by the cord of nourishment and life that held her securely to her mother's body. She didn't even wonder how she knew that her name would be Angela; somehow she just knew. She had been floating like this each day for the past six months as she listened to the soothing, reassuring beat of her mother's heart. There was never any fear or any hunger. Angela only experienced the feelings of safety, satisfaction and peace.

As Angela brought her hand up to place her tiny, little thumb in her mouth, something began to change in this serene environment of hers. She felt a burning pain start to cover her entire body, starting at her feet. What was happening? Angela had never experienced pain before, but suddenly the pain was unbearable. Why was this happening! Why wasn't her mother stopping whoever was inflicting this incredible pain.

Angela opened her mouth as if to cry out in protest, as bit by bit the burning spread over parts of her body. But what was never heard was the silent screams of this unborn child.

Chapter 1

The day was cold and rainy outside and as Dr. Ben Strictland sat and listened to the man delivering his daughter's funeral service, he felt as if the cold and rain had reached into his very heart and soul. The funeral home was full of friends and family. His wife, Julie, sat beside him with tears streaming down her face. Ben didn't even begin to know how to comfort her because he could find no comfort for himself. He couldn't even seem to cry; he just felt this overwhelming emptiness and anger.

He barely heard the words that were being said. They didn't mean anything anyway. How could they? This man, standing up there saying all those patronizing words about his daughter, hadn't even known his beautiful little girl. He had never seen her dimpled smile as she looked adoringly up into her father's eyes. This man had never felt the warmth of her hug when she was tucked into bed at night. Now he would never experience those wonderful moments again either. The realization of this came rushing over him like a tidal wave and it was almost more than he could bear.

Julie reached over and placed her hand in his, and as he squeezed her cold, trembling hand, he let his mind travel back through the years to that night long ago when they had first met.

They met at a fraternity party while in college. She was just a Freshman and he was in his Senior year. Normally, he wouldn't have even given a Freshman a second glance, but something about this tall, graceful young woman intrigued him from the very beginning. She had long, jet black hair. She wore it straight and pulled back from her face, which made her enormous blue eyes look even larger. She had a smooth creamy complexion and wore hardly any makeup. That was one of the first things that attracted him to her, that natural beauty. She stood there in a group of people, quietly listening to all that was going on around her. She had an air of self confidence and at the same time seemed so soft and vulnerable. Every now and then something would strike her as funny, making her cheeks dimple and a smile would brighten her whole face.

He had slowly made his way over to the group of people she was talking to and as several of the group left to get something else to drink, he introduced himself to her. As he talked to her, she gave him her full attention. She didn't just pretend to be interested in what he was saying, she really listened. He found himself talking much more than he usually did and before he knew what he was doing, he had asked her out for the following night. That was the beginning of his relationship with Julie. They began dating and dated steadily throughout that year.

Julie filled a void in his life that he had not even realized was there. He was the only child of parents who had never seemed to have the time for him. Oh, they were nice to him, in an off handed sort of way, like he was one of their many possessions. Since they made plenty of money, he was given whatever he wanted, but they were so caught up in their jobs and social life that he seemed to be an afterthought most of the time. He remembered how he had resented them for this. Growing up, he had often wondered why they had even had him, since their lives seemed to revolve around everything but him. When he was younger, he had craved their attention, often irritating them rather than receiving the love and warmth that he desired. As he grew older, his resentment and anger toward them grew and he quit vying for their attention and just did his own thing.

But Julie, she was different. He had felt from the very beginning that she truly cared for him. They could talk for hours or just sit quietly and enjoy each other's presence. They would be in a crowded room and her look would make him feel as if he were the only one there that really mattered. Julie was a very affectionate person and an impulsive hugger. She had a theory that when people hugged, their bodies gave off chemicals that made them happier, healthier people. Ben was in pre-med and he had never heard of this, but he enjoyed her hugs so much that he wasn't about to dispute her theory. She had filled his life with so much joy and love that he never seemed to get enough of being around her. That whole year was filled with a happiness that he had never experienced before. They ate together, studied together, went to social events together. Sometimes they would just take long walks, hand in hand. However, the year had come to an end all too quickly.

When he had received the letter accepting him into medical school, he hadn't known whether to jump for joy or sit down and cry. Julie was on a full scholarship studying music. She had such an amazing musical talent that he didn't want her to give up her studies. He felt that she was a great pianist and he wanted her to finish her degree as much as she did. However, the medical school at which he had been accepted was 800 miles away and he could hardly bare the thought of leaving her. They discussed it every day for the next week and finally decided that there was no other solution but for him to go on to medical school and her to stay there and finish her music degree. He would have liked to marry her right then and to have taken her with him. However, he knew how much time and energy med school would take and he didn't want her to give up her scholarship. Her family did not have a lot of money and she had worked hard to even be able to attend college.

During the last month of school, they had spent every moment that they could together. His parents had come for his graduation, but it was Julie's face that he had looked for in the crowd after he accepted his diploma. He and Julie had dinner with his parents that night. He remembered being glad that they had to leave immediately after dinner to go back to their respective jobs. He had been very upset with them for basically ignoring Julie during dinner and drilling him about what his plans were for the summer. He was also glad for them to leave early because that had been he and Julie's last night together. Julie would be going back to her parents to work for the summer and he would be going to Houston to work and get settled before med school started in the fall. He had planned to visit her for a few weeks and meet her parents toward the end of the summer. However, they both knew that after that, they would only be able to see each other during holidays, at the most once or twice a year. He remembered feeling at that time that the pain of leaving Julie was surely worse than anything he would ever have to experience again. He'd had no idea how minor that pain would be in comparison to what he was feeling now. After all, he had been sure of Julie's love. He had known that even though they would be apart and would not get to see each other often, she would continue to love him and they would spend their lives together.

So the next day, with tears in their eyes, they had parted. They were apart two months before Ben visited her at her parents. Those two months had seemed like an eternity. She had written and he had called a lot. He had never been much of a writer. She had seemed so excited about him meeting her family each time she wrote.

Julie had three younger brothers and a younger sister. Her brother Tommy had been sixteen at the time, Carl was twelve, Stephanie was ten and David was six. They all lived in a very small house on the outskirts of Chicago. Ben had been surprised at just how small and old their house was. Oh, it was clean and cheerful, but the furniture was old and worn and there was only one full bathroom for all those adults and kids. Their lives seemed so busy and happy, but he could tell they had struggled financially in a way that he had never had to experience.

Ben learned to love Julie's family during those two weeks and he felt that they had accepted him and maybe even grown to love him. After a few days, as he became caught up in all the family fun and activity, he forgot how small the house had seemed to him initially. He especially liked David who seemed to want to follow him around everywhere. Stephanie was very quiet and shy, but he could tell that she adored Julie and wanted to be just like her. Carl was in that awkward stage of puberty and talked all the time. Tommy spent most of his time with his friends so Ben didn't see too much of him. Julie's father, Richard was a tall, large man and her mother, Sandra was short and petite. They were so relaxed and comfortable with each other and were always showing their affection by a touch on the hand, a hug or just a special look that they had for each other. They were so unlike his parents, who never touched or showed affection in public. Ben could easily see where Julie got her warm ways. As busy and hectic as it always seemed to be at their house, they all made an effort to sit down at the dinner table together.

He had made up his mind about one thing during that visit, however. He wanted to give Julie all the things that she'd never had growing up. He wanted to finish medical school and his residency and he wanted to become a successful doctor so that she would never lack for money again. He also made up his mind that no matter how painful it would be to be separated from Julie, he would not marry her until he had finished medical school and his residency. He didn't want their lives to start off with them having to struggle to make ends meet and he certainly didn't intend to accept any money from his parents. He had decided in his mind that she'd had enough struggle growing up and he wanted to wait until he could give her the kind of house and the kind of things that he wanted her to have. It never once crossed his mind, back then, that she'd had so much more than he had as a child, even with his parent's abundance of money. She'd had the love, security and feelings of self-worth that all of his parent's money had never been able to buy him. But because of his love for her and because growing up, all he had been able to measure his parent's love by were the things that they had bought him, he was consumed with the desire to provide all that he could for her. He was so grateful for her love, a kind of love that he had never experienced before and he wanted so much to give her everything in return. If possible, he wanted to help her family, someday as well.

Chapter 2

Medical school was a lot harder than Ben had imagined. Making good grades through high school and college had always come very easy for him. He had studied some but that didn't even compare to the time and effort he had to put in that first year of medical school. From the very beginning he realized that it was going to be very competitive and that it would indeed take most of his time and energy to do well.

He and Julie talked weekly and he loved getting the long, newsy letters that she sent him each week but he was glad of their decision to wait to be married. He needed to keep his mind focused, so he could get through this first year. Four years had seemed like such a long time when he and Julie parted that summer, that they decided to think of one year at a time and concentrate on doing their best during that year. Besides, he would see her at Christmas and he was so busy, the time truly did seem to fly by. Even though the hours were long and the professors demanding, he loved those first months of medical school. However, by the time Christmas vacation came around, his grades were good and he needed the long awaited break.

His parents planned to be abroad during Christmas and Ben had been invited to spend Christmas at Julie's house. He had a two week break from school and had missed her so much. He hadn't even had time to do any shopping but decided that it would be more fun to shop with Julie anyway. That way he wouldn't have to carry the gifts on the plane. He wanted to get each member of her family something very special. He was sure she could help him find just the right thing for each of them.

Julie was waiting for him at the airport. The minute he stepped off the plane, he saw her anxiously watching for him and as their eyes met, her face dimpled into that heartmelting smile. As she ran toward him, she threw her arms around him in one of her "healthy" hugs. Oh, how he had missed those hugs. Maybe there was something to her theory about hugs after all. Her's sure felt good to him now. After smothering his face in kisses, she took both his hands and stepped back, looking him over from head to toe. As they walked toward the baggage claim area, Julie exclaimed over how tired he looked and how she was going to spend the whole two weeks pampering him and making sure that he got plenty to eat and plenty of rest.

However, rest did not seem to be in the picture. When they arrived at Julie's house, everyone was busily involved in Christmas activities. David ran out the door as soon as they pulled up in the driveway and grabbed his hand asking him all about what being a doctor was like. He laughed and explained to him that he wasn't a doctor yet; he was just learning to be one.

He had forgotten how small her house was but what he had not forgotten was how comfortable they made him feel. They were all happy to see him and exclaimed over how glad they were that he was able to spend Christmas with them. They all seemed to talk at once, asking him all about his first months in medical school. What always amazed Ben is that they truly seemed to want to know. Even Tommy seemed more interested this time.

Their house may have been small but it was beautifully, decorated for Christmas. It was very different from how his home had been each year at Christmas. His mother had always decorated to perfection. Everything had to match and most of the decorating was done by Emma and Herbert, an older couple that lived on their property and did the cooking, house cleaning and yard work. Julie's house was decorated with a lot of homemade garlands and ornaments and the smells that continually came from the kitchen made Ben's mouth water.

He hadn't even thought about his meals at school. He was always so busy, he just ate out of habit, most of the time at odd hours. For the first time in months, he found himself looking forward to each meal. Meals at the Bennett house were an event in themselves. They ate at a big country table in the kitchen and there was always plenty of food and plenty of talk.

As Ben sat there eating dinner that first night, he wondered how his parents would have reacted to a meal with the Bennetts. Meals at his house had always been such a formal affair. They always ate in the dining room at a table much too large for just three people. The table was always impeccably set with the best crystal and china and served by Emma, their housekeeper. There was talk at their table also, but it never seemed to include him. Whenever he tried to enter the conversation, his parents would just brush off what he had to say and continue with their talk about their jobs and social functions. He had finally learned to eat in silence. But that was not the case at Julie's. They included him in every conversation, asking his opinion and wanting to know all about what he had been doing the last few months.

He and Julie shopped two days before Christmas. It had taken them nearly all day to find just the right presents for everyone. Julie had waited to do her shopping with him. He bought David a game that Julie said he wanted, Stephanie a small gold bracelet, Carl a new baseball glove and Tommy some of his favorite cologne. It took him a long time to decide on a gift for Mr. & Mrs. Bennett. He finally bought them a VCR, which Julie told him was entirely too extravagant but he noticed that they didn't have one and he really wanted to get it for them. He and Julie split up, one going one way and the other going the other way in the mall, to buy each other's gifts. He found exactly what he was looking for after about an hour of looking in half the jewelry stores in the mall. Julie wore her hair pulled back most of the time and he found her a beautiful pair of small, but elegant pearl and diamond earrings.

Christmas Eve and Christmas Day were unlike any Ben had ever experienced. On Christmas Eve they had their meal and then everyone got to choose one present from under the tree to open. They were all so excited and couldn't decide which one to choose. David chose the one from Ben and jumped into his lap and gave him a big hug when he opened the game. Neither he nor Julie chose the one from each other but instead, chose a gift from one of Julie's brothers and sister. He received a paperweight from David that he had made in school and Julie opened Stephanie's, which was a little book of poems that Stephanie had written. Julie was very touched by it. She gave Stephanie a big hug which made her blush and beam with happiness. After everyone had opened their gifts, David wanted them all to play his game with him. They laughed and talked until it was time for the younger children to go to bed.

He and Julie did get a few minutes alone together that night. He missed time alone with her but he did enjoy her family. They bundled up and took a long walk in the snow. They didn't even talk very much but just walked hand-in-hand enjoying being close to each other.

The next day started bright and early. David woke up around 6:00 a.m. and that meant everyone else was awakened. By the time all the presents were opened, there was no room to move for all of the gifts and paper. Everyone loved their presents. Julie's parents didn't know what to say about the VCR. They were so surprised and kept saying, "This is just too much Ben." Julie had tears in her eyes when she opened her earrings. Ben could tell that they were just the right gift for her. They looked beautiful on her. She had given him a lovely sweater and he had put it on immediately after opening it.

After stacking all the gifts in separate piles and clearing away all the paper and boxes, they sat down to a wonderful Christmas meal of turkey, dressing, sweet potatoes, green beans, yeast rolls, mashed potatoes with gravy, and so many choices of deserts that Ben had to have a little of each. That night they watched two movies they had rented and ate turkey sandwiches and more sweets. It had truly been a wonderful day.

The two weeks seemed to fly by. It was the best Christmas Ben had ever experienced. He had gone back to school excited about getting back to his studies but a little melancholy about leaving this place that made him feel so loved and important.

Chapter 3

The winter and spring quarters seemed to fly by and Ben finished that first year at the top of his class. He spent a lot of time that summer with Julie and her family. By the end of the summer, they were even closer and he felt more and more a part of her family. When his vacation was over, it was very hard to buckle down and start his second year of med school.

Once he got started, however, he was once again engrossed in his studies. The only time he got to see Julie that year was at Christmas break when he again spent Christmas with her family. By the time that year was over, he was relatively sure that he wanted his field of medicine to be in Obstetrics and Gynecology. He had worked in the different areas of medicine that year and still had Pediatrics and the Emergency Room to experience, but he was definitely leaning toward OB/GYN. He was intrigued with the study of hormones and he liked the fact that the majority of the patients in this field were healthy, instead of all being ill. He also felt that bringing life into the world added some balance to the illness and death that most doctors are faced with day after day. Of course, gynecology had its share of illness and problems also, but at least there was a balance. He would have to decide by the middle of his third year. He had talked with Julie about his decision the past summer. She seemed excited that he was interested in that field. She loved children and had been excited that Ben would want to bring life into the world. She had jokingly said "By the way, it will come in handy when we have our children." He had changed the subject quickly, at the time, because to him children were in the very distant future, if at all. He sometimes wondered if it was even a good idea to have children, the way things were in the world at that time. Being a father also scared him because he had no idea how to be a good one and he did want to be a good father, if they had children. He also wanted to have the time to spend with them and as a doctor, especially an OB/GYN doctor, his time would not be his own.

After spending time in Pediatrics and ER, he definitely decided to go into the field of OB/GYN. He declared this field by the end of his third year and his fourth year was spent focusing on that decision. Once he had made his choice, his last year of medical school seemed to fly by.

He ended up with very good grades and would start his residency at the hospital in Houston in September.

It had been four, long, hard years and even though he had been extremely busy trying to not only to keep up with but to compete with the other medical students, he had missed Julie immensely. The only times they had been able to see each other were during Christmas vacation and during the Summer. However, their relationship had continued to remain steady and their love had flourished, despite the years of separation. In fact, the thought of Julie had gotten him through many sleepless nights of study.

Julie would not be able to attend his graduation, as she still had two more weeks before her own. He planned to leave immediately after he graduated and fly in for hers. His parents had promised to be there to see him graduate, but as he looked for them after the ceremony, they were nowhere to be found. When he got back to his apartment, they had left a message on his machine that they had been called out of town on business and would not be able to make it. Ben thought how typical this was of their interest in all of the important events of his life. He wondered if they would find the time in their busy schedules to even make it to his wedding when he and Julie finally did get married. In a way, he almost hoped they wouldn't be there because Julie's parents were so different, it would probably only cause conflict. Besides, he was sure that Julie's parents did not have the money to give her the kind of wedding that his parents would expect.

All of these thoughts and resentments toward his parents played havoc with his mind the first hour of his flight, but then he began to relax and anticipate his reunion with Julie. Ben could hardly wait to see her and feel her in his arms.

He arrived at the university the day before her graduation. Her family had a room at The Ramada Inn nearby and they had booked a room for him as well. Julie was so excited to see him! It never failed to amaze him that this beautiful, vivacious, young woman could love him as much as she did. The night before her graduation, they went out to dinner alone. They had spent the whole afternoon with her family, which had been full of noise and fun as usual, but finally they were alone. Julie had not seemed her normal, bubbly self most of the afternoon, but after they had ordered, Ben looked over and saw tears about to spill from her eyes. "What's wrong, Julie?" he had asked with a knot of fear forming in his stomach. "I don't know," Julie had responded. "It has just been such a long four years and now I am graduating and hope to find a teaching job soon and you've graduated from medical school. Can't we finally get married and be together? I know you want to wait four more years until you finish your residency and get established in a practice, but Ben, I need to be with you. Can't I apply for a teaching position in Houston and we could be together. I just don't know if I can stand being apart for four more years." By then, Julie was sobbing and quickly left the table for the ladies room.

Ben sat there, trying to think of all the reasons why they should wait, but all of a sudden he couldn't remember any of the reasons he had come up with before. All he could see were those tears flooding down Julie's cheeks and he knew that he no longer wanted to wait either.

It seemed like forever before Julie finally returned to their table. He was almost ready to go into the ladies room to make sure she was alright. Her eyes were red and puffy but she had stopped crying. She looked very embarrassed, as she said, "Ben, I'm sorry for that outburst. I know you have our best interest at heart, it's just that these last four years have seemed so long and...." Ben gently put his finger over her lips, stopping her long enough to tell her that he no longer wanted to wait either. All those reasons didn't seem so important anymore. "All I wanted," he tried to explain, "was to be able to give you a nice place to live and to be able to provide for you properly when we got married. I never meant to hurt you. It's just that my time was not my own during medical school and it will be even worse during my residency. Even if we are married, I won't be able to spend much time with you." Julie assured him that those things made no difference to her. All that mattered was that she would be there for him when he could be home. The rest of that evening had flown by, as they excitedly discussed Julie flying back to Houston with him to look for a teaching job and to start planning their wedding.

They told her family the next day during breakfast. Ben had been worried that they might object, but they were all talking at once, they were so excited. Ben tried to explain to them that they didn't want to wait for a big wedding and that maybe they should just find a quiet place and get married, as soon as possible. However, the look of disappointment on her mother's face made them both reconsider. They discussed it for a while and compromised by deciding that Julie would fly back with Ben, for a week, to apply to schools in Houston for a music teaching position and then fly home to help her mother plan a small wedding for the beginning of August. That would give them a week for a honeymoon and then a few weeks to settle in before Ben started his residency.

Julie's graduation was exciting for her whole family. She was their firstborn and to have her graduate from college was a big event for her parents. Ben had never seen her look so beautiful. He sat there and wondered how he had ever thought he could wait four more years to marry her, when he wasn't even sure he could bare waiting until August.

They spent the next day with her parents talking about all of the things that needed to be done between then and August. The whole family took Ben and Julie to the airport the next morning, wishing her luck with her job applications and promising to see Ben soon. Julie talked the whole flight to Houston. Ben had never seen her so excited. He could have sat beside her all day listening to her talk and laugh.

Ben decided to show Julie all that he could of Houston on the first day and then take her to the schools in the area to pick up applications the day after. By the end of the week, she had applied to five schools and was assured that she would know something by the middle of July. It had been a wonderful week. They both felt as carefree and happy as little children! Neither of them had studies waiting and they both had graduated with honors. It seemed like, for the moment, the burden of studies and responsibilities had been lifted from their shoulders and they could just enjoy themselves. They looked at apartments the last few days of the week and finally put a deposit down on a small, two bedroom apartment near the hospital where Ben would be doing his residency.

While Julie had been interviewing for jobs, Ben spent some time shopping and on Julie's last night in Houston, he pulled out a big package for her to open. She opened it very slowly, wondering what it could be and when Ben could have bought it. Her mouth opened in a silent gasp as she pulled out a beautiful cobalt blue, silk dress. It was the prettiest dress she had ever seen. Ben told her to hurry and get dressed because he was taking her to the fanciest restaurant in town. She went in one bathroom to shower and dress and he went in the other.

It was a night she would remember and cherish the rest of her life. They went to L'Auberge, an elegant French restaurant. Ben ordered for them and they had lobster bisque, a wonderful spinach walnut salad, tenderlion in a white wine sauce with steamed vegetables. For desert they had bananas foster, prepared at their table. During dinner, a man went from table to table playing beautiful, romantic violin music. After he had played a special song for Ben and Julie, Ben pulled a small square box from his inside coat pocket. He got down on one knee by the side of her chair and asked her to do him the honor of becoming his wife. As tears flowed down her cheeks, he put the most beautiful diamond solitare on her finger and everyone in the restaurant applauded. Julie laughed and cried at the same time as their waiter brought them a bottle of champagne to celebrate.

Chapter 4

The day of the wedding dawned bright and clear. Ben woke up very early, thinking about the night before. The rehearsal dinner had gone better than he had expected. His father's and mother's attitudes had actually been pleasant when he picked them up at the airport. He could sense that they were still upset with him for waiting until a month before the wedding to tell them about his engagment to Julie, but they didn't let on around Julie's family that they were upset. He wasn't sure if they were upset about the late notice or if it was because they didn't approve of Julie.

The rehearsal dinner was at a local Italian restaurant. A private room was set up and there was a buffet of several pasta dishes, a salad bar, french bread and a choice of lemon pie, apple pie or cheesecake for dessert. Ben knew when he picked this restaurant that it had very good food but was not elegant, by any means. He knew that his parents would have picked something a lot more sophisticated, but Italian food was Julie's favorite and somewhere in his mind, he rebelled against choosing a place he thought they might have chosen. Besides, the wedding was to be very simple, with a reception at a nearby Hampton Inn and Ben didn't want Julie's parents to feel that his family was trying to outdo them in any way. He wanted everything to be perfect for Julie's sake.

Everything did go well that night and the next day was as close to perfect as it could get. Ben had a late breakfast with his parents. They didn't make too many comments about the night before. They did say that they thought Julie was very attractive in an unpretentious way and that her family seemed very nice, but extremely large and talkative. Ben caught himself about to come to their defense and then decided to avoid conflict at all cost in order to keep the day as pleasant as possible.

His father told him that they had been trying to decide on an appropriate gift and that they would like to send them on a honeymoon trip to the Bahamas. Ben told them that they had planned to spend the night in the Hyatt Regency, outside of Chicago and then they were taking their time driving to Houston, as their honeymoon. He could tell that his father was about to get upset again, so he quickly told him that they could save the trip for a celebration gift when he finished his residency. This seemed to appease them both and the talk turned to his residency.

His father began to drill him on why he had picked OB/GYN for his field of medicine. He tried to explain to them his reasoning but his father kept pointing out all the negatives, such as being called in at all hours because of deliveries and the high cost of medical insurance in that field. Ben just let him talk and as soon as the meal was over, he excused himself, telling them that he had several things to attend to before the wedding. He told them he would meet them in the lobby at 1:00 to go to the church together.

He really didn't have much of anything to do. He had already booked the hotel and had arranged to have flowers and a bottle of champagne in the room. He ended up just taking a walk by the water for a few hours, thinking of Julie and how he wanted their life to be together.

The ceremony was beautiful. The chapel was small but had stained glass windows on all sides depicting the four seasons of the year. Ben stood at the front of the chapel, while the groomsmen ushered in the bridesmaids. All of Julie's brothers and sisters were in the wedding. In fact, Tommy was his Best Man and Stephanie was Julie's Maid of Honor. Then, all was quiet, as the organist began the wedding song. Ben looked back at Julie standing there with her father and his heart swelled until he thought it would burst. She was absolutely breathtaking. She had on an ivory colored gown of satin and antique lace. The sun was filtering through the stained glass windows and it seemed as if she was stepping through a rainbow of colors. Her hair, her face, her dress, everything was a vision of beauty. He could hardly believe that in a very short time, she would be his wife and they would share the rest of their lives together.

He hardly remembered what the minister said as they repeated the traditional vows. As Julie repeated hers, her face dimpled into that smile that had captured Ben's heart five years earlier. She didn't even seem nervous, while he was so nervous, he thought his legs might not hold him up. Finally, the minister pronounced them husband and wife and he took Julie into his arms and kissed her.

They stayed at the church for pictures to be taken and then rode to the reception with her parents. It seemed like the reception would never end. Ben was so anxious to be alone with Julie. There had been so many people around all week and so much to do, that they had barely spent any time alone together. Quite frankly, he would have rather eloped but he knew how important this wedding was to Julie and her family. They danced, ate cake and talked to more people than he ever cared to know. Then, finally, it was time for them to change out of their wedding clothes and they were on their way.

They had packed Ben's car the day before and only had a twenty minute drive to the Hyatt. That was a night that neither of them would ever forget. It was incredible knowing that they were finally husband and wife and they would never have to be separated for long periods of time again. Ben didn't realize then, that time and space were not the only separators of people.

It took them five days to drive to Houston. They slept late each morning and stopped along the way, at any place that caught their interest. They had three weeks before Ben started his residency and Julie would start teaching at a local high school one week after that. Ben had driven this route many times over the last four years, but he now noticed places and things that he had never noticed when driving alone. Julie took an interest in everything around her and they were constantly stopping to see something of historical interest, to shop, or eat in some quaint little place that Julie just had to see. The five days seemed to fly by as they spent every moment together, driving, talking, sightseeing, planning their future, and learning even more about each other than they already knew. Ben wished that this time could go on forever, because he knew, even more than Julie did, how hectic their lives would be after he started his residency.

They arrived in Houston on August 18th. They had to pick up the key to their apartment from Mrs. Spencer, the manager, before her office closed. She was a sweet, plump, little gray-haired lady, probably in her seventies. Her eyes had a twinkle in them as she told them how glad she was that the newly weds had finally arrived. Ben could tell that Julie took to her immediately. She reminded him a little of Julie's grandmother. She told them that she had put a welcome box of goodies on their kitchen counter and that they should let her know if they needed anything else.

They were both anxious to get into their apartment after traveling for a week. Ben unlocked the door and ceremoniously carried Julie over the threshold. The apartment was empty but they both stood there for a while in each other's arms, just enjoying the sight of their first home together.

They finally broke apart and started carrying their meager belongings in.

After about two hours of this, they decided to try to find a good place for dinner, as they were both famished. The goodies that Mrs. Spencer had left for them included a loaf of homemade bread and some other homemade sweets, but they were hungry for something a little more substantial. They discovered a great little Chinese restaurant, about a block from their apartment and they both ate more than they thought possible for just two people, especially since they had eaten some of Mrs. Spencer's cookies earlier.

That night, they slept on the floor, as they had no furniture in their apartment. The first thing on their agenda the next day was to shop for furniture, especially a bed. Even though the floor was carpeted, it did get rather hard by morning. They stopped by Mrs. Spencer's apartment after breakfast, to ask her if she knew of a place to find some good, sturdy, inexpensive furniture. She told them of several places and by the end of the day, they had purchased a bedroom suit, an oak table and four chairs, a navy, green and burgundy plaid sofa bed, with two navy overstuffed chairs, two oak end tables, a coffee table, three lamps and a desk and chair for the second bedroom. Their final purchase had been a piano. Julie had received the money to buy a piano for a graduation present and had decided not to purchase one until they were married and moved into their own home. This took them the longest to shop for, as it had to be just the right one. Julie must have played two dozen before finding the one that she wanted. They had received all of the dishes, kitchen appliances, towels and sheets that they thought they would ever need for wedding gifts.

Ben was not a shopper at heart, but he actually had a great time with Julie that day. They were totally exhausted by the end of the day and still hadn't bought any food to prepare for dinner. They ended up eating out for dinner again, even though Julie had wanted to have their first meal in their own home that evening.

Most of the furniture would be delivered the next day, but they had managed to coerce the man at the furniture store to deliver the bedroom furniture that evening. After finding sheets and a blanket among their boxes, they made the bed and fell, exhausted onto the mattress. Ben was too tired to even get under the covers. He never realized moving into an apartment could be such an ordeal. He had rented a furnished apartment while in medical school and didn't really care what it looked like as he spent most of his time in classes or studying at the library. Married life was certainly going to be different. All it took was Julie snuggling up close to him and him smelling her wonderful, fresh, scent to know that even though it would be different, it would be exactly what he had wanted his whole life.

They spent the rest of that week arranging their apartment, unpacking and getting to know the area a little better. By the end of the week, their apartment looked very nice. It was amazing what a woman's touch could do. Ben remembered thinking how much their little home reminded him of Julie's house and how little it reminded him of his. That's exactly how he wanted it. He wanted that same warmth and love that surrounded her parent's home and family to be a part of theirs.

The three weeks seemed to pass too quickly and it was time for Ben to start his residency. They were both looking forward to this next step in their lives, however. Monday morning found them both up early. Julie had fixed a nice breakfast and gave him his health hug for the day. They kissed lingeringly at the door before Ben left to start his career as a doctor. Never were there two more optimistic people.

Chapter 5

Julie spent that first week of Ben's residency putting the final, finishing touches on their apartment. She bought curtains for the bedroom and kitchen. She got Mrs. Spencer's permission and stenciled sea shells around the top of the wall in the bathroom. She bought some material and made throw pillows for the couch and their bed. She was having so much fun decorating that the week flew by and she hardly noticed the long hours that Ben put in at work.

She also put an ad in the local paper advertising private piano lessons. She and Ben had decided that since he would be spending so much time at the hospital, maybe private lessons, along with her teaching would provide them a little extra income and give her something else to occupy her time. In her own mind, she also wanted to get a base of piano students started, so that when they decided to have children, she could stay home with them and not resume teaching in school until their children were old enough to start school.

Julie and Ben had not talked too much about children. She wanted a large family, but every time she brought up the subject of children, Ben seemed to get very nervous and change the subject. He did tell her that he wanted children but somewhere in the distant future. He wanted his practice to be well established and he wanted them to have some financial security before bringing children into the world. It sounded like a poor reason and too long a period to wait to Julie. When he saw the disappointed look on her face, he also told her that he wanted some time for just the two of them before starting a family.

Julie loved her teaching job. She would bubble over with excitement when Ben did make it home from the hospital, which wasn't very often. His schedule was even worse than he had anticipated. It seemed as if he ate, drank and slept the hospital. His work was very stimulating and interesting and he was learning so much, but he was tired all the time. Julie seemed to handle his absence well. When he would finally get to come home from the hospital, she would greet him at the door and treat him with such tenderness and care, that it was like finding an oasis in the desert. She was always eager to share about her students, especially the ones that seemed gifted musically, but she was also anxious to hear about his patients and his day at the hospital.

Julie was an excellent cook and she seemed to enjoy trying special dishes out on him when he was able to be at home. He had to admit that most of it was very good, even though he had to ask what some of it was. It certainly beat the cafeteria and vending machine food that he had eaten when he was in medical school. But better than the food was the fact that he knew Julie would be there waiting for him when he finally did get home. That first year was one of the happiest he could ever remember. They were both were extremely busy, but so happy with one another.

Ben was able to be off for one week that summer and after Julie ended her first year of teaching, they decided to fly to Chicago, to spend a week with her family. She asked him if he didn't want to see his parents, but he assured her that they were too busy and probably wouldn't be in town the week they had planned to take off anyway. Julie tried not to question him too much about his parents. He remembered when they were dating, that she couldn't understand why he never wanted to take her to visit his parents and spend time with them. He had explained to her then that they were so caught up in their own lives that they never seemed to care about his anyway. She had seemed puzzled and hurt at the time, but she just didn't understand because her family was so different. She had gotten along amazingly well with them at their wedding and had commented afterwards that she liked them. Julie corresponded with them that first year of their marriage. He didn't understand why because they hardly ever wrote or emailed back. They would call once every few months, but the conversations were always formal and stiff. They seemed to laugh and talk more freely with Julie, however, than they ever had with him, but then everyone loved Julie.

They left for Chicago the Monday after Julie's school term ended. She was so excited, she could hardly sit still in the plane. She hadn't seen her parents since their wedding and she had so much to share with them. She had taken pictures of the apartment so that her parents could see where they lived and how she had decorated. She also took some pictures of her favorite students from school.

Ben was just glad to have a week off. He was so exhausted from the crazy hours he had put in the last year. In fact, as soon as the plane got up into the air, he was fast asleep and slept until they touched the ground in Chicago. Julie let him sleep, even though what she really wanted to do was talk about their trip. She truly did seem to understand how much his residency was taking out of him. She told him that he could sleep late every day if he wanted and that she would make an effort to keep her family as quiet as possible and let him get some much needed rest. He didn't want to spend their whole week sleeping however. He had missed her family also and he hardly ever got to see Julie. He decided that if he could just take that first day and sleep, he would be caught up. Then he could participate in the fun and craziness that was always a part of visiting her family.

Her parents, brothers and sister were all at the airport to meet them. Thus began the round of hugs and kisses. They had to drive two cars so everyone could fit and still have room for their luggage. Julie's dad said he had tried to leave all the kids at home but they would have none of that. They were all too excited about seeing Ben and Julie. Julie's mom commented on how tired he looked and told him they would try and let him get some rest.

Julie must have kept them all out of the house for two days, because other than meals, he seemed to sleep the majority of those first two vacation days. After that, he felt human again and really enjoyed sharing about his patients and playing with David. He and Julie managed to get in some time with just each other also. Her parents seemed to sense that they didn't get much of that at home. They did some sight seeing and went out to dinner several times. The Saturday before they left, they packed a picnic and loaded up the two cars and went to a nearby park for the day. All in all, it was a wonderful week and he went back to Houston refreshed and ready to start again.

Julie increased her number of private piano students during the summer, since school was out and she had a lot of free time. She tried to work her students around Ben's schedule, so that when he was home, the music lessons would not disturb his much needed rest.

The summer went by quickly. Julie spent a lot of time out of doors. She helped Mrs. Spencer plant flowers around the apartments and did some local sightseeing. Toward the end of summer, she began to prepare for the school year ahead. Her extra private students wanted to continue during the school year, so it seemed as if the next year was going to be very hectic for her as well.

Each day seemed to get busier and busier the second year of their marriage. He could tell that his continued absence was starting to get to Julie. They hardly ever got to see each other. He worked sometimes 24 hours a day and when he was home, he was so tired that he would fall asleep as she tried to share her day with him. She was trying so hard not to complain and to be understanding, but he felt the strain.

He planned to take a few weeks off after he finished his second year of residency and they were going to take that honeymoon that his parents had wanted to give them for their wedding. He felt as if he really needed some time alone with Julie, away from the hectic pace of their lives. Julie was so excited about the idea of having him all to herself. That seemed to get her through the last months of that year. Actually, it's what got him through also. They had decided to go to St. Thomas in the Caribbean. Julie had never been out of the United States and was extremely excited about their trip. The next weeks seemed to creep by.

Finally, the day arrived for them to depart. Julie hadn't really known what to pack, so she packed far more than Ben felt they needed. However, he had been so busy that he hadn't had the chance to talk about the trip with her very much. He was just glad to be getting away from the hospital for a few weeks.

Ben listened to Julie talk for about ten minutes once they were on the plane and then he was fast asleep. Julie was so excited that she could hardly stand to have him sleeping beside her when there was so much she wanted to talk to him about. However, she knew how tired he was and wanted him to get as much rest as possible at the beginning of their trip, so he could enjoy all the sights with her. She had been so starved for his company this past year. She had known that he would have to spend the majority of his time at the hospital but they were newly married and she felt so isolated sometimes. Her family was very far away and at times homesickness would almost overwhelm her. If they were nearby, at least she would have been able to visit and talk with them. She had so much, each day, that she wanted to share with

Ben and if he did come home at all, he was so exhausted he would fall asleep in the middle of her conversation.

Julie was thankful for her students. She had thrown herself into her work and music these last two years and did feel some sense of accomplishment and worth from that. Some days she loved being married and sharing her life with Ben and some days she felt as if she wasn't married. Their lives, so far, just didn't fit into her vision of what married life would be like. She did love Ben with her whole heart and couldn't imagine life without him. She just hoped it would be different once he was finished with his residency. She really felt that this vacation would give them a chance to renew their intimacy and relationship with each other.

Their flight was a long one and Ben slept through most of it, while Julie sat there and daydreamed about their upcoming romantic days together on the island.

When their plane landed, it was already dark but Julie could tell that this was a beautiful place. They rented a car at the airport and drove to the hotel where Ben had made reservations. Julie was astonished. She had never seen such a luxurious hotel. They had a suite of rooms with a balcony that overlooked the ocean. There was a plush sitting area with bright floral furniture, a wicker table and chairs and a bar area, with a refrigerator and an assortment of drinks and snacks. There was a beautiful bouquet of roses and a bottle of champagne that Ben had called ahead and arranged. It was all so beautiful and romantic, that it wiped away any hurt feelings that had been forming over the lack of time she and Ben had spent together the past year. This was going to be such a wonderful two weeks! She could feel that already.

She immediately ran out to the balcony. She couldn't see the ocean very well in the dark but she could hear it and smell it and stood there just soaking in the sound. To a musician sounds are very important and this was truly music to her soul.

Ben followed her out on the balcony and putting his arms around her, pulled her close to him. He always loved the smell of her. It was like walking through a garden of new spring flowers. He was so tired but just holding her and feeling her near him seemed to revive him in a way nothing else could. They ordered room service that night and enjoyed the food, champagne and each other.

They slept until almost noon the next morning and Ben awakened feeling more refreshed than he had in a year. Julie was already up and in the shower. He could hear her singing. He could tell that she was happy and he wanted that more than anything else. He knew that she had been feeling down lately because of their lack of time together. She tried not to show it and she never complained to him but he hadn't seen that sparkle in her eyes lately, not until last night. As much as he resented his parents money sometimes, he was very thankful for this trip. He planned to spend every minute of it making Julie happy.

After they were both showered and dressed, they went down for lunch in the hotel. Then they decided to ride around and tour the island for the afternoon. Julie had fallen in love with the ocean. The day was sunny and balmy. They stopped and explored some of the beautiful blue beaches and tropical areas. They decided that they would spend each morning on the beach and then explore more of the sights each afternoon.

One afternoon they went snorkeling. Julie loved the many colored tropical fish. It was like swimming in a fish tank. They would come up and nibble at your fingers and toes. They went horse back riding on the beach one after-noon. Each night they tried different restaurants on the island. Julie tried many new foods that she had never tasted before. She was just like a little child let loose in a giant toy store. Everything was so new and exciting for her! Ben found himself anticipating every night the things he would show her the next day.

They had a lot of time to talk and really shared with each other in a way that his schedule had not allowed in the last year. Julie did tell him that he was gone much more than she had imagined he would be, before they were married. She knew he couldn't help that but it was so hard not having someone to share her thoughts and feelings with most of the time. In a family as large as hers, there was always someone to talk to. She explained that it was just very different than what she was used to or had expected.

Ben tried to assure her that things would change after he finished his residency. He really wasn't so sure that was true because of the field of medicine he had chosen. In fact, Julie had asked that very question, wondering if his time would ever be his own, as an OB/GYN doctor. He promised her that somehow he was going to spend more time with her once he had a practice established.

She didn't seem to care that night as she snuggled up close to him. She was just happy about the time they were spending together. However, Ben lay awake that night thinking of their discussion. He wanted so much to make her happy. This was the very thing he had been afraid of when he had wanted to wait to be married. He truly believed that he would be able to establish a good enough practice, that he would eventually have the money to make more of his time his own.

The rest of that week was one of the best times he could remember. He felt as if he and Julie were closer than they had ever been before. He loved his work, but he almost wished their time here would never end and he and Julie could just stay on this island, away from the stress and fast pace of normal life.

The two weeks did end, however, and as they left the beautiful island Julie had tears in her eyes. Ben couldn't understand why she was crying; they'd had such a wonderful time. She explained that's exactly why she was crying because they'd had so much fun and she knew they had to get back to the reality of her teaching music and him spending long hours at the hospital. There was nothing he could do about his schedule, so he just held her close and assured her that he would do all he could, after his residency, to have more time with her. Ben felt as if the vacation had drawn them closer than they had been in a while and he wanted very much to keep that closeness, despite his hectic hours at the hospital.

Chapter 6

B en jumped back into his work with renewed vigor after their two weeks in St. Thomas. He felt refreshed and ready to attack his grueling schedule once again. He did love practicing medicine. He didn't really mind the long hours because they seemed to fly by while he was at the hospital. Every case was new and different and he learned so much each day. Learning about medicine in school and actually practicing medicine were totally different. The only thing he minded was not being able to spend enough time with Julie. Sometimes he almost felt guilty for enjoying the time at work so much.

This year he would be spending all of his time working with the OB/GYN doctors on staff at the hospital. He was really excited to start spending all of his time in the field of medicine that he had chosen.

Ben liked the doctors he worked with. Dr. Williams was a little obnoxious and joked around about his patients more than Ben thought appropriate but the other two, Dr. Johnson and Dr. Weaver, were very serious about their work. They were all very good doctors and Ben felt that he would be able to learn a great deal from them the next two years.

The days and weeks seemed to fly by. Ben tried to be more alert when he came home and to listen to Julie about her day. She seemed to really enjoy hearing about his days at the hospital and about his patients. She especially liked to hear about the deliveries and how many babies were born each day.

Ben could see the yearning in her eyes, sometimes, when he talked about the deliveries. He knew that she really wanted children but he couldn't even think about that yet. He barely had time to give Julie all that she needed as a wife; he sure didn't have time to be a father. He did think that he wanted children one day but not until he had more money and more time. He wanted to be able to concentrate on getting through this next year and a half of residency.

One thing happened during that year of his residency, that he was never able to share with Julie. In fact, he was never really able to get it totally out of his mind. Ben would never forget that day, sixth months into his third year of residency. He knew that abortions were rarely performed at the hospital, and therefore he had never assisted in one. That morning he had arrived early at the hospital and Dr. Williams was going over the surgeries scheduled for that day. One of the patients was a young woman, Sabrina Long, who was well into her fifth month of pregnancy before deciding she did not want the baby. They were doing the abortion at the hospital instead of the local abortion clinic, because she'd had some prior heart problems. Ben asked Dr. Williams why she had decided so late not to have the baby and he said it was because her husband had left her and she didn't feel she could raise the baby by herself. Ben knew that the later into the pregnancy abortions were performed, the more chances for complications.

Ben didn't really know a lot about the doctor's lives outside the hospital and hadn't known that Dr. Williams performed abortions on a regular basis until that day. When Dr. Williams saw how uncomfortable Ben looked as he discussed the abortion scheduled that day for Mrs. Long, he laughed and explained to Ben that it was a simple procedure.

Besides, if the mother didn't want the baby, it was better not to bring it into the world. There were enough unwanted children in the world already. Ben still felt uncomfortable but thought about how his parents had never taken much interest in him and decided that maybe Dr. Williams was right. Maybe unwanted babies were better off never even entering this world.

The abortion was scheduled for 1:00 that afternoon. They had a hysterectomy that morning and several women were in the labor rooms waiting to deliver. He helped Dr. Johnson deliver a baby at 11:30 and then had time for a quick lunch, before the scheduled abortion. But, for some reason he didn't seem to have an appetite. He ate some crackers and a soft drink and then went to scrub and get ready for the procedure. Dr. Williams was in talking with Mrs. Long and then came in to scrub and get ready.

Ben walked into the room and looked at the young woman laying there on the delivery table. He introduced himself and he could see tears forming in the corners of her eyes. He asked her if she was okay, as he tried to busy himself with the instruments. She admitted that she wasn't sure. She had wanted this baby but then her husband left and she didn't want to bring a baby into the world, not knowing if she could provide for it. She told Ben that she already knew it was a girl and that she even had a name picked out, Angela. Ben asked her if she was sure this is what she wanted. As tears seeped from her eyes she nodded a "yes" just as Dr. Williams entered the room.

Dr. Williams had chosen to inject a saline solution into the placenta which would burn the fetus, causing it to abort. In all of medical school and his residency thus far, Ben had not actually seen an abortion performed. Dr. Williams finished scrubbing and came into the room to begin the procedure. He explained what he was doing each step of the procedure. He explained that the fetus would be more developed than most he aborted, but that once the saline solution had covered the fetus, it would abort naturally. The most disturbing part to Ben was when the saline solution was inserted. He could actually see the mother's stomach move as the fetus struggled frantically in the uterus.

Ben felt that there was nothing natural about the procedure. When the fetus aborted, it wasn't just tissue. It was a little baby girl, completely formed but very tiny. She was burned over most of her body but her little face hadn't been touched by the saline. It would have been easier to handle if it had been burned also but the pain on that little face was clearly visible. He had almost lost it. It was so horrible to him at that time. He did manage to stay in the room for the whole procedure but he then left as quickly as he could.

As he finished rounds that afternoon with Dr. Williams, he tried to put the abortion out of his mind, but kept seeing instead that little baby girl's face. He thought about all of the babies he had helped deliver in the last six months and what a wonderful thing the birth of a child was. He kept telling himself that this was a legal procedure and that a woman should not have to have a child if she didn't want to. Besides, if a child was not wanted, it was better off never coming into this world.

Dr. Williams noticed that Ben was preoccupied most of the afternoon and after rounds were over, he asked him to go to the cafeteria to get some coffee with him. He re-emphasized to Ben that the abortion had gone well and that the mother had no complications. He told him that it was just a fetus that was unwanted by the mother and that legally, that was her choice, not theirs. Ben told him that it was easy to say it was a fetus, but it looked like a baby to him.

He asked Dr. Williams how long he had been performing abortions. He told him that he had started out doing a few here and there, for his patients at the hospital and then he had been asked to work at a local abortion clinic two days a week. He had decided to do it because there was so much money in it. It was an easy procedure and because of the additional money, he was able to free up two afternoons a week to play golf and spend time with his family.

Ben asked him how he could deliver babies part of the week and then abort them the other two days of the week. Dr. Williams explained to him that he just had to get past seeing them as babies. They were not babies to him until they were full term, delivered and breathing. In the early stages of pregnancy they were just tissue and he was removing the unwanted tissue from the mother. He told Ben that he would not do it if it were illegal but that the mother had a right not to carry that child for nine months if she didn't want to. He also told Ben that some of the doctors working in abortion clinics were not trained in obstetrics and that he felt women were better off having someone trained to know what to do if there were complications.

He did tell Ben that this baby today was much further along than normal. He had estimated five months but it was closer to six. Still he justified it because it was the mother's choice.

Ben still could not get over the look on that little baby's face or the look on the mother's face right before the abortion. He decided, however, that it was over and done with and he would just put it out of his mind. He finished his afternoon by throwing himself fully into his other patients and his work.

He did have to struggle with the thoughts again that afternoon while helping with another delivery. As he saw this new healthy little girl come into the world, he couldn't keep the thought of that other baby girl out of his mind. He stayed busy all afternoon and went home that night completely worn out.

Julie asked him about his day and his patients. He told her about each one, except he couldn't bring himself to talk about the abortion. He had decided that Dr. Williams was right, it was the mother's choice, not his, or any other doctor's. They were just there to help their patients in any way they could and they had helped this patient. He wasn't going to think about it any more.

That was easier said than done for Ben the next few weeks. He dreamed about the baby girl that night. She was a perfectly formed little baby and as she was being pulled away from her mother, she was looking straight into his eyes and crying, "Help me, please help me!!!!" He woke up in a cold sweat. Thank goodness he hadn't awakened Julie. She still slept peacefully beside him. He got out of bed and went and got a drink. He turned the TV on to try and get his mind on something else. After about an hour, he went back to bed and finally went to sleep.

He had to consciously keep putting the thoughts out of his mind. Thoughts of the abortion would continue to pop into his mind all week. In fact, he had nightmares two more times. One time the little baby was lying on a blanket and Dr. Williams was pouring gasoline over it. Right before he lit the match, the baby looked at him in agony and cried, "Please don't let him hurt me! Please save me!" Every time these dreams came, or thoughts came during the day, he went over in his mind all the reasons that abortions were okay. It was his patients' best interest that he should have at heart not this unborn fetus.

After a few weeks of consciously deciding that what he had been a part of was okay, the thoughts and dreams began to slowly stop haunting him. He had finally justified it in his mind. He didn't think any child should come into the world feeling unwanted, as he had. He finally convinced himself that it was the best thing for the mother and the baby. He didn't even realize that in this thought process, he had admitted it was a baby.

The rest of that year seemed to fly by. Ben's work consumed more and more of his time. Something seemed to happen to Ben after that abortion experience, however. He had never shared the experience with Julie but she could tell that he seemed different in some way. They talked and shared their days during the brief time that they had together but he had closed off a part of himself. There seemed to be some kind of distance between them that she couldn't put her finger on. Ben could feel it also, but he would have never admitted that it was because of that first abortion.

He had assisted Dr. Williams in several other abortions since then. but they had not affected him like that first one They were earlier in the pregnancy and he had managed, after struggling with himself over that first one, to numb any feelings he had about them one way or the other. He simply looked at it as another procedure that he was learning in the process of becoming the doctor that he wanted to be.

Julie, however, worried daily over the distance that she felt. They talked and loved and shared with one another but something was missing. She talked with her mother and father weekly and that helped her not feel as lonely. She had made several friends among the teachers at school and they went and did things together sometimes. She worked to make their apartment as clean and pleasant as possible but that hardly took any time, it was so small.

She decided at the beginning of Ben's last year of residency, that she would add more private students to her teaching schedule. He never seemed to be there anyway and she needed to fill her time with something.

She loved her students. Some were not very talented musically, but worked hard at learning. She did have a few private students that showed a lot of talent. Some days, as she worked with them, she wondered what their children would be like. She knew that Ben didn't want to even talk about having children until he finished his residency and was established in a practice, but she longed to have a baby. She believed that would fill up some of the loneliness that continued to creep in. She didn't understand how Ben could deliver babies everyday and not have a longing for one of his own. She did believe, however, that Ben eventually wanted children and she was prepared to wait.

Chapter 7

That summer Ben had two weeks off. Julie rearranged her private students and he scheduled his vacation so that they could go back to Chicago for Tommy's wedding. It hardly seemed possible that he was twenty-three now. He had finished college the year before on an ROTC scholarship, with a degree in Engineering. He had been commissioned into the Air Force out of college as an officer. He was stationed in California but was flying back for the wedding. He was marrying a young woman he had been dating since his senior year in high school. The whole family was very proud of him.

Carl was nineteen, working part time and going to a local community college at night. Stephanie was seventeen, finishing her last year of high school and it hardly seemed possible, but little David was now thirteen. Ben could tell that Julie missed her family in a way that he couldn't understand. He missed them also, but he knew that Julie stayed homesick most of the time. Sometimes he would find her with tears in her eyes when he came home at night. She would brush them away and act like nothing was wrong, but he knew differently.

Julie suggested that they take the other week and visit his parents. They hadn't seen them since their wedding. Ben didn't really want to see them, but she kept insisting that it wasn't fair to always visit her family and never visit his. Ben reluctantly called to see if they would be in town that week and to his dismay they said they would. They even seemed excited about their visit. To himself, he thought they would probably call and cancel at the last minute, but surprisingly they didn't. They were going to go visit his parents first and then go to be with Julie's family, in time for the wedding.

As the time approached to leave Houston, Ben became more and more nervous. He didn't know why his parents seemed to always have this affect on him. Julie could sense his nervousness as she sat beside him on the plane. She tried to keep the conversation light and pleasant and hoped that he would at least try to get along with his parents. She was actually anxious to spend some time with them. She called or emailed them more often than Ben knew about and she was hopeful that they were beginning to form at least a friendly relationship.

They were very different from her family but they were polite and interesting to talk to. Ben fell asleep during most of their flight, but awakened about fifteen minutes before their plane touched down. His nervousness had changed to grumpiness. He found himself being short with Julie as they waited for their luggage. He had thought that his parents would at least be there to meet them at the airport, but instead they sent their driver, John, to get them. Julie was chatting away and trying to ignore his attitude, but nothing she did seemed to cheer Ben up. She finally gave up and just sat there in silence as they rode toward the Strickland's home.

Julie was beginning to get a little nervous also. She had never been to Ben's house. He had never talked much about the way it looked, just that it was big and unfriendly. As the silence continued in the car, the knot in her stomach began to grow.

Ben sat there feeling bad for biting Julie's head off in the airport, yet feeling this anger that he could never seem to define as they rounded the corner to his parent's home. He looked over at Julie and saw her mouth drop open as they approached the house. It did look enormous at night, with all the lights on. She reached over and grabbed his hand and said, "I had no idea it would look like this!"

John drove to the front door and told them to leave their luggage and he would see that it was brought in. Anna met them at the door and told them his parents were waiting for them in the library. Julie was taking in every inch of the foyer, from the shiny marble floors to the huge chandelier. She had closed her mouth at this point, but Ben could tell she was in shock.

She still clung to his hand as he led the way to the library. Julie had never known anyone whose house had a library. She loved to read and as they entered the room lined on three sides with beautifully bound books, she thought she must have died and gone to heaven. There was a fireplace on the back wall as you entered the library, a huge oak desk to one side and a soft coffee colored leather sofa in front of the fireplace with two wingback chairs on either side. There were beautiful Persian rugs on the hardwood floors. The whole room had a soft welcoming look with the smell of leather in the air. It was a completely different atmosphere than the lavish look of the entry way.

Mr. & Mrs. Strickland stood to welcome them. Mrs. Strickland hugged Ben and Julie and gave them a quick peck on the cheek and Mr. Strickland shook Ben's hand and hugged Julie. They asked about their flight and if they wanted some refreshments before dinner was served. Ben told them they weren't hungry; they'd had a snack on the plane. Mrs. Strickland laughed and said, "How can you endure that airplane food. When James and I travel, we used to have Anna pack us a little snack. Now we have to buy something in the airport as they won't let us take our own food on the plan anymore." Ben rolled his eyes as he looked at Julie. Julie just smiled her big, dimpled smile that would melt the coldest heart and said that they didn't want to spoil their appetites before dinner.

Mrs. Strickland offered to show Julie their room, so she could freshen up a bit before dinner. Ben told her that he was perfectly capable of taking them to their room himself and that they would unpack and then he would show Julie around the house before dinner. His mother looked taken back but agreed that they would see them at dinner at 7:00 sharp. Julie followed Ben out of the library. She wasn't sure whether to say something to Ben or not. She felt that his attitude toward his parents was totally uncalled for. In fact, he seemed to be a totally different person from the Ben she knew. She decided to keep silent until they were in their room.

They were in a huge bedroom, with a vaulted ceiling and a beautiful crystal chandelier. The walls were a light yellow, with white trim. The floor was a beautifully stained, hardwood, with a soft colored Persian rug. The bedroom furniture was a dark cherry and there were two antique, green velvet chairs in front of the fireplace. The bed was covered in a soft white on white silk comforter with embroidered edges and an embroidered dust ruffle. The whole atmosphere was sunny and cheerful yet rich and luxurious. It sure didn't fit Ben's mood.

They unpacked their bags in silence. Julie took her toilet bag to the adjoining bathroom. It was amazing. It had two beautiful, handpainted sinks with bronze fixtures and an old clawfoot bathtub. There was a shower as big as their apartment's bedroom. The whole bathroom had the atmosphere of a luxurious spa.

As she came back into the bedroom, Julie wasn't sure what to say to him, but finally asked why he had been so short with her in the airport and so rude to his mother a few minutes before. He was silent for a moment, because he wasn't sure he knew himself. He tried to explain to her that his parents just always seemed so artificial to him, especially compared to her family and that something about being here just brought out the worst in him. He told her that growing up, he had felt so alone here. His parents were either gone all the time or too busy for him when they were at home.

She went over to him and put her arms around his neck. She looked him in the eyes and told him that he would never have to feel alone again because she would always love him and be with him. He hugged her close to him and tried to absorb all the love and warmth that he could get from her. He kissed her and apologized for being gruff with her and even for being short with his mother. He promised her he would make an effort to be pleasant and nice to his parents and to try and have a good time while they were there. He took her hand and said, "Now come on and I'll show you the rest of this monstrosity before it's time for dinner."

As they walked into the hall and started their tour of the house, he wondered what he had ever done to deserve someone like Julie. She had enough love and warmth in her to make even this old house seem friendly.

They toured the upstairs first. There were six, big bedrooms, each with its own bath and sitting area. There was a wing for Anna the housekeeper and John the chauffer. His parent's bedroom suite was downstairs. Their bedroom suite alone was almost as big as Ben and Julie's apartment, with a fireplace in the bedroom and the bathroom. There was a media room with theater chairs, a soft leather couch, and a huge flat screen television, a sunny breakfast room, a huge modern, state of the art, kitchen, an enormous dining room with a table big enough to seat twenty people, and the library, which was Julie's favorite room. The last room they entered was a large formal living room, which had the most beautiful grand piano Julie had ever seen.

She went over and sat on the bench and ran her finger's across the keys reverently. Ben encouraged her to play and she asked if he was sure it would be okay. He told her that no one played it, unless they had a party and they had someone in to play background music for the entertainment. She couldn't believe that someone would have a piano like this and not play it.

She had been working on writing a song, that she planned to play and sing at her brother's wedding. Ben hadn't heard it yet. In fact, no one had and she decided to try it out on him and see what he thought. He was amazed. The song was a love song about the union between husband and wife and as he sat and listened to her play and sing, tears came to his eyes. It was as if she had written it for him, instead of her brother. He never ceased to be amazed at her musical talent.

Toward the end of the song, his mother and father came into the room and even they were impressed. They told Julie that they had no idea she could play and sing so well. She blushed and they asked her if she would play something else. She played a few classical songs and Ben could tell that his parents were amazed and impressed. They knew that she taught music but they were surprised at her ability. They asked her if she would play some for them each day while she was there and to feel free to use the piano any time she wanted. Julie thanked them and told them what a lovely house they had.

Mr. Strickland suggested that they all go in to dinner, as it was almost seven. Julie thought they would eat in the breakfast room or kitchen, since there were only four of them, but the table was formally set in the dining room. Julie sat across from Ben and Mr. and Mrs. Strickland sat on either end of the table. It seemed as if there were miles between them. Everything was so formal. There was a beautiful floral arrangement in the center of the table, almost too big to even see Ben and two silver candleabras. Anna served them a shrimp cocktail appetizer to begin with. Then, they had a salad and a light cucumber soup. Next came the main course.

They had sliced pork tenderloin, covered in a burgundy mushroom sauce, wild rice, asparagus and wonderful yeast rolls. They ended the meal with chocolate mousse. Julie was so full, she thought she might not be able to get up from the table. This was certainly not the kind of meal she and Ben ate at home. They usually ate light at night because it was sometimes 10:00 or later when he got home from the hospital. It took them almost two hours to eat.

Mr. and Mrs. Strickland asked Julie about her music and how many students she had. Julie eagerly responded to all their questions and went on and on about some of her students. It amazed Ben that she seemed to draw out his parents in a way he never could. They did ask him about his residency and he told them a little about the doctors he was working with and some of his more interesting cases.

His father, being a lawyer, warned him again about the high number of malpractice suits in his field of medicine and asked him if he was sure that he had enough malpractice insurance. Ben assured them that he had as much as he could afford at the time. "I still don't know why you chose obstetrics," his father commented. "You were in the top of your class out of medical school and you could have chosen any field you wanted." Ben's face turned red as he said, "That is the field I wanted, father." There was an uncomfortable few moments of silence and finally Julie broke it by telling them all about their apartment and some of the friends she had met and worked with at school. Ben's mother tried to get into the conversation with Julie and act interested, but his father and he just sat there in stony silence.

Finally, the meal was over and Ben told his parents that he and Julie were going to take a walk around the grounds. He actually thought they seemed relieved that they didn't have to entertain them anymore. His mother said they were a bit tired and they thought they would just retire to their suite. They would see them at breakfast the next morning.

Mrs. Strickland said that breakfast would be served at 7:30, as Mr. Strickland had to be in court by 9:00. She invited Julie to go to a Cultural Arts meeting with her at 10:00 the next morning. Julie told her she would love to attend and looked over to see Ben glaring at her.

They walked outside in silence. The grounds were beautiful and Julie breathed in the fragrant air. They walked past a beautiful pool area and onto a garden path. There were many different kinds of flowers in bloom. Julie asked Ben who kept up their flowers so beautifully and he told her they had a gardener who worked full time on the grounds.

Julie could tell that he was upset about something, so they just walked along in silence for a while. Ben finally turned to her and asked her why she had told his mother she would go with her the next morning. "I don't know what you mean." stated Julie. "I thought it would be a good chance to get to know your mom a little better. Why would that upset you." "I'm not upset," snapped Ben. "I just know my mother and she'll want you to go with her to all of her little social functions every day. I thought this was our vacation and that we would spend time together."

Ben knew that he was being childish but it really bothered him that his mother would invite Julie to go with her, without thinking that he might want to do something with Julie. He wouldn't examine his feelings deep enough, to realize that he was jealous because his parents had never seemed to want him to be a part of their social life and yet, right off the bat, his mother invited Julie to go with her.

Even though Julie didn't understand Ben's reaction at all, she told him that she wanted to spend time with him but that she would also like to get to know his parents better. She promised him that she would only go to this one function with Mrs. Strickland and then she would spend so much time with him that he'd probably get tired of her. That made him laugh and relax a little. "You know that I never get tired of being around you," he said. "In fact if you weren't here, I wouldn't be able to stand to be here right now."

That really bothered Julie. She wondered what she could do to get Ben to loosen up around his parents and not spend the entire week with this sullen little boy attitude. "Ben," she asked "Can't you just try harder to get along with your parents and not take offense to everything they say to you." "Well, if they would say something positive every now and then, instead of finding things wrong with everything I say or do, I might be able to," Ben responded in a brooding tone. "Julie, my parents never took an interest in me. They were always too busy from the time I was a little boy. Anna would read me a story and tuck me in bed at night. Half the time, my parents weren't even home at night. When I got older, they were never there for any important event. They would say they would try to come and then never show up. They weren't even there when I graduated from medical school. You don't understand, Julie. Your parents are completely different."

Julie hurt for the little boy in Ben but she very patiently took both his hands and looked him in the eye as she said, "Ben, all that doesn't matter now. You have done great things with your life. You will soon be a doctor practicing medicine on your own. You are one of the finest, most caring people that I have ever known. I love you with all of my heart. You have so much to be thankful for. Why can't you just be secure enough in all that to not need so much from your parents now. Maybe they don't know how to give you what you need and they may never be able to do that, but you're okay just the way you are. If you can get to that point and just try and love them anyway, then maybe you can have a different kind of relationship than you've ever had with them before."

They sat there under the gazebo in silence for a while holding hands. Ben really thought about what Julie had just said. Would he always have this deep, empty space that needed to be filled by their love? Wasn't Julie's love enough? She was proud of him and that should be enough. If he could just stop expecting things from them that they never gave, maybe he would be happier. He decided that the rest of the week, he would work on feeling good about himself, no matter what they said and love them, expecting nothing in return.

He leaned over and gave Julie a long, lingering kiss. "How did you ever get to be so smart," he asked? She just smiled and with her arms around his neck kissed him softly on the lips. They sat there talking a while longer and then decided to go back to the house and watch TV a while in the den. They cuddled up on the couch and Julie was soon fast asleep. Ben looked down at her and the love he felt for her just swelled up inside him. He woke her gently and they went upstairs to bed.

Ben and Julie were used to getting up early. So they had no problem being in the dining room by 7:30 for breakfast. There were a variety of choices on the sideboard. Breakfast was a kind of help yourself affair. Anna made sure everyone had all the juice and hot coffee they needed. There were scrambled eggs, biscuits, bacon, potatoes and fresh fruit. There was also cereal for anyone that wanted a lighter breakfast. Julie never seemed to have to watch her figure. She never gained weight, no matter what she ate, so she piled her plate high. Breakfast was her favorite meal of the day.

Mr. Strickland, who was just having a bowl of cereal and a piece of toast looked at Julie's plate as she sat down at the table and chuckled, "My, young lady, you certainly have a healthy appetite." Julie turned red and commented that the food all looked so good she couldn't choose what she wanted so just got some of all of it. She asked where Mrs. Strickland was and James said that she was sleeping a little late because she had a headache and wanted to feel better before her Cultural Arts Meeting.

Breakfast was a rather quiet meal. Mr. Strickland read the paper as he ate and Ben seemed rather quiet. It still seemed strange to Julie to sit at such a large table with so few people. She smiled as she thought about how her family would have filled up this table and how noisy it would be in a week, when they visited them. Even though it was quiet and she seemed to be the only one in a good mood, she ate her food with gusto. She wasn't sure what to expect from this Cultural Art affair that she was going to with Mrs. Strickland or how long it would last but she wouldn't have to worry about getting hungry.

Ben sat and ate his breakfast in silence. He looked down the long table at his father reading the paper and remembered many silent breakfasts as a child and how he would hurry and eat his meal so he could leave the table. His mother's headache this morning was not unusual. She had always seemed to find a reason not to join he and his father for breakfast. There had never been friendly chatter in the morning or anyone there to kiss him goodbye before school or wish him a happy day. Then he looked over at Julie, with a smile on her face, enjoying every morsel of her food and he couldn't help but smile. She was so different from his family. He wondered what it would have been like if he'd had a brother or sister. Maybe life wouldn't have been so silent and lonely.

When he and Julie did have children, he wanted to have at least two or three, so they wouldn't feel the loneliness he had growing up. Of course, he knew that he and Julie would never allow a child of theirs to feel like he had as a child. She looked up at him just as she was putting a piece of pineapple in her mouth and gave him her dimpled smile. The gloom seemed to leave his heart as he smiled back at her.

His father folded his paper as he got up from the table. "Well, Ben, Julie, I'd better be going. I have a full day in court. You two have a nice day and I'll see you this evening at dinner." Julie thanked him and Ben just sat staring across the table wondering what had brought on that friendly departure.

As Julie finished eating, she started to clear the table out of habit. Anna bustled in saying, "NO, NO," Ms. Julie! You mustn't do that! You just go have a good day. That's my job." Ben smiled and took Julie by the arm as she started to protest. He told her that Anna would be offended if she stayed to help her.

He led her to the library and they browsed through the books for a while. Ben showed her some of his favorite books as a child and she picked out a few she would like to read while they were there. She asked Ben what he would do while she was gone with his mother and he said he thought he would drive into town and do a little shopping. He had a few things he wanted to get before they went to her house next week. Julie told him that she would like to shop one day also, as they still had to get Tommy a wedding gift. Ben promised her that they would go another afternoon. He told her that if she got back in time that afternoon, maybe they could go for a swim in the pool before dinner.

Julie went up to their room to decide what to wear to this meeting and to get ready, so she wouldn't keep Mrs. Strickland waiting. Ben stayed down in the library to read the paper; a luxury that he very seldom had time for at home.

Julie decided on a coral, linen dress that had short sleeves and very plain lines but could be dressed up or down, as the occasion warranted. She wore a gold chain and bracelet and small gold hoop earrings. She worried and fretted in front of the mirror, not even realizing how stunning she looked. She went back down to the library to wait for Mrs. Strickland and when she walked in, Ben gave a low whistle. She blushed and smiled, asking him if he thought this outfit would be sufficient. He assured her that she would be the most beautiful and sophisticated looking woman there. She laughed, and said that she felt anything but sophisticated.

They talked for a while, until Ben heard his mother enter the room. "Well, Julie, my dear, are you ready to go? My don't you look lovely," was her only comment. Ben walked them to the car that John had waiting in the driveway. John opened the door for them and Ben kissed Julie goodbye and whispered, "Good luck," in her ear.

The meeting lasted from 10:00 to 12:00 and had really been rather interesting. Julie loved the arts and could tell that Mrs. Strickland was highly regarded among the other members of the committee. Most of their talk centered around fund raising for the local theater and art gallery.

After the meeting, Mrs. Strickland suggested they go to the Country Club for lunch. Julie wasn't sure how Ben would react to missing lunch with her also, after his mood last night, but she hadn't had much time to visit with Mrs. Strickland and she wanted to get to know her better, so she told her that she'd love to.

The club was very elegant and they had a wonderful lunch. Mrs. Strickland asked Julie a lot of questions about their lives in Houston and her teaching job. She truly seemed interested, so Julie told her all about their apartment and how it was close to the hospital. She talked about her students at school and some of her private students that seemed to be very talented. As she talked, Mrs. Strickland asked her to please call her Margaret from now on and she commented on how amazed she had been the evening before when she heard Julie play the piano. She asked Julie why she hadn't pursued a career as a concert pianist. Julie was very flattered and went on to explain that when she first entered college, that had been her desire but after she and Ben had meet her first year in college, she had known that what she really wanted was to be his wife and share her life with him. She told Margaret that she loved children and that teaching was very fulfilling to her. "It's just a shame to waste all that talent," Margaret sighed, "and I don't know how you have the patience to put up with all those children."

Julie could have taken offense, but she wanted to know why Ben's mother felt that way about children. Maybe it would help her understand Ben's childhood better. "Margaret, I feel as if I am using my talents in a much more productive way than I would have as a concert pianist. I'm able to help children develop what talent they may use someday for that very reason. Don't you like to be around children?"

"Children make me nervous," Margaret stated. I was an only child and I've just never felt comfortable with them. When Ben was born, I had never been around babies and I didn't have a clue what to do. I became so agitated that James hired a nannie and she took care of Ben most of the time until he was old enough for school. By then, James was so involved in his law practice and I in my work and charities that we just left him mostly to himself. He was such a quiet child and never seemed to require much attention."

I knew after I had him that I didn't want any more children. They just make me too nervous. I guess I'm just not the motherly type. I loved Ben, but after he entered high school and then went to college, we grew further and further apart and it was harder to relate to him. I thought it would be easier as he got older, but it never has been."

Julie wasn't quite sure what to say. She couldn't comprehend not liking children, but in a way she felt sorry for Margaret. She seemed to want to relate to Ben, now that he was an adult but he had shut her off since she had deprived him of that relationship as a child. Julie told her that maybe if she tried talking to Ben more and taking an interest in his life now, he would respond and they could build a closer relationship. "It's so much easier talking to you," Margaret confided. "Ben just clams up when he's around us. There's always strife between he and his father and he takes everything we say the wrong way." "Just be patient with him and persistent," Julie urged. "If you continue to show an interest in his life, I'm sure he'll respond eventually."

Margaret changed the subject at that point and started telling Julie about her latest fund raising ideas. Julie tried to be interested in what she was saying but her mind kept wandering back to the conversation they had just had. She really wanted Ben to be able to grow closer to his parents, for his sake, as well as theirs. They finished their meal and when they left the club, John was there to drive them home.

That afternoon, Julie and Ben swam and sat by the pool and read as they soaked up some sun. When Ben asked her how her day with his mother had gone, all Julie would say was that it was very interesting and that she felt she understood his mother a little better. Ben just snickered and said, "I'm glad you do because I never have." Julie urged him to just give his parents a chance and try not to be so negative towards them.

The rest of the week went by quickly. They swam and read and relaxed. It was very pleasant to Julie, and Ben even seemed to be having a good time. He and his parents didn't argue any more and they all seemed to be trying harder to get along. The meals were wonderful. Anna was an excellent cook. It was so different for Julie to be waited on hand and foot. She wouldn't want to live her life that way but it was kind of nice for a week.

As they packed to leave for the airport, Ben pulled Julie to him and thanked her for helping to make the week so pleasant. He told her that this was probably the nicest time he had ever had with his parents. Nothing he could have said would have made her happier. She kissed him a long, lingering kiss, so he wouldn't see the tears that had formed in her eyes.

Mr. and Mrs. Strickland hugged them goodbye and urged them to visit again soon. It was a completely different atmosphere than when they had arrived. John drove them to the airport and on the way Ben sat quietly at first. Then he spoke up and told Julie that his parents had never hugged him goodbye like that before. It hadn't been a drastic change but there was a difference in the feelings that were there. Maybe the fact that there had been any feelings at all was what was so different. Ben puzzled over it all the way to the airport.

Chapter 8

B en and Julie both slept most of the way to Chicago. Ben was surprised that Julie slept since she was so excited about seeing her family. They had shopped some while at his parents and had bought Julie a new dress for the wedding and him a new suit. They bought Tommy and Ashley, his fiance, a nice toaster oven for a wedding present. It was hard to believe that Tommy was in the Air Force and getting married. Time did seem to go by quickly.

Julie's father and David were the only ones at the airport to meet Ben and Julie this time. Richard apologized that everyone had not come but explained that things were rather hectic at the house, as the wedding was in two days. David talked to them non-stop most of the way home. He told them all about Junior High School and the sports he had been involved in during the previous year. Ben still had a special place in his heart for David and even though David was a teenager now, his adoration for Ben had only grown over the years.

Everyone ran out to hug them when they arrived at the house. As usual, everything was noisy and fun. They had a big family dinner that night and Ben and Julie got to meet Ashley for the first time. She was petite and cute, with short, auburn curls that fit her pixie personality. She was perfect for Tommy and she and Julie hit it off immediately. They had so many people at the dinner table that it could hardly hold them anymore. Ben wondered what they would do as the family continued to grow. He thought about the meals he and Julie had just shared with his parents and how big that table seemed with so few people around it. He was so thankful to be a part of this big, boisterous, happy family and he was looking forward to the day that he would be well established in his practice and be able to not only provide things for Julie but also be able to help her family more.

They finished eating and then Ashley and Julie helped Mrs. Bennett clear the table and do the dishes while the rest of the family went into the den to watch a movie. It seemed that the VCR was a much used and appreciated gift. They all stayed up much too late but they had so much catching up to do.

Ben slept late the next morning while Julie went with her mother to get some last minute things for the wedding. That night was the rehearsal dinner and the wedding was the next day at 11:00. It was a small wedding and the most beautiful part to Ben was when Julie played and sang the song that she had written for Tommy and Ashley. As it had the first time, it again brought tears to his eyes.

The reception was simple but elegant as theirs had been and they all ate and danced and had a wonderful time. To Ben it seemed like a balm after the week with his parents. Granted he and his parents had gotten along better than they probably ever had before, but still he always felt apprehensive around them. At the Bennetts he could totally relax and enjoy himself. Julie seemed to be in her element also. He could tell that she had really missed her family. Everything had been focused on the wedding their first three days there as it should have been, but Ben was anxious to just be able to visit and catch up on things the remainder of their stay.

They all slept late the next day and just relaxed most of the afternoon. Julie's father had the week off and they planned to go to a local amusement park later in the week, which David was really excited about. Other than that, they didn't really do a lot. They just wanted to relax and visit, which is exactly what they did.

The week seemed to fly by and before they knew it, they were on the plane flying back to Houston. As usual, Julie was teary eyed most of the flight back. Ben had learned over the last few years that when she was like this the best thing to do was to not say anything but to just hold her hand and let her feel his love. In a way he understood, but not totally. He knew that she missed her family and that her life in Houston was lonely a lot of the time because of his work schedule. She constantly told him how much she loved him and he knew that she did, but he was so looking forward to this last year of residency being over and getting started with his practice, wherever that might be. He truly believed that he would have more time with Julie then.

Chapter 9

Things got back into some sort of routine as Ben started his last year of residency and Julie went back to teaching her music students. This year was a very important one for Ben, as he would be deciding what to do after his residency was finished. He couldn't afford to start his own practice yet, so he was hoping for offers from some of the doctors in the area to join their practice. He had a feeling that Dr. Williams or Dr. Johnson might offer him a place in one of their offices.

This last year was a time when Ben would fine tune his skills as a doctor. A lot of the procedures that he had merely assisted in over the past three years, he was now doing on his own. He loved his work. The only part that he didn't particularly like was the fact that they did do abortions periodically. These did not bother him the way that first one did, but each time he assisted in one, he would have that same dream about the first little girl he had seen aborted. He had not performed one on his own yet, but one was scheduled for later in the week.

Julie noticed that Ben seemed troubled or preoccupied that week, but whenever she tried to talk to him about it, he just assured her that it was fatigue and nothing else. Ben wished he could tell Julie about how that first abortion had affected him. Then, maybe he would stop dreaming about it but Julie didn't even know he assisted with these abortions and he knew that she would not approve. The one time he mentioned the subject, she had become very upset and said that she didn't understand how anyone could ever kill a little baby. He had tried to explain to her that it wasn't a baby yet, just tissue, and that it should be the mother's choice but she was so adamant about her feelings, that he quickly changed the subject.

The night before he performed his first abortion himself, he woke in a cold sweat, after having that same haunting dream. He was able to go back to sleep after a while but he had to really talk to himself the next morning and reassure himself that performing an abortion was perfectly legal and it was in the best interest of the mother and the child, if the child was unwanted. He got through the procedure just fine and kept himself very busy the rest of the afternoon so that no stray thoughts could enter his mind.

Ben performed three more abortions before that year was up and each time it got a little easier and his conscience bothered him a little less. The dreams had even started to subside. Besides, he told himself that he had no choice during his residency. He simply had to do what he was instructed to do by the other doctors. He assured himself that after he went into practice he would try to avoid this one unpleasant part of his chosen field of medicine.

That year flew by. As the last month of his residency drew near, Julie became more and more excited. She truly believed that Ben would have more free time when his residency was over and she told herself that maybe, then, they could talk about having a child.

Different thoughts were crowding Ben's mind however. He'd had an offer from both Dr. Johnson and Dr. Williams and could not make up his mind which to accept. He had discussed it with Julie, but she didn't really know either of them and told him that he should just weigh the pros and cons of each and make his decision based on that. He really respected Dr. Johnson more as a doctor, but the offer from Dr. Williams had been a better one financially and the sooner they were in better financial shape, the sooner he could give Julie all the things he wanted her to have, starting with a house. Also, Dr. Johnson already had two other doctors in the practice with him and Dr. Williams only had one other, Dr. Harvey.

After actually putting down the pros and cons on paper, Ben let his desire for more financial freedom get the better of his knowledge that Dr. Johnson was by far a better and more ethical doctor. He assured himself that Dr. Williams was a fine doctor also and he had offered him the better deal. He told Julie about his decision and that next day, two weeks before he finished his residency, he accepted the offer from Dr. Williams and declined the offer from Dr. Johnson. For some reason, after he had made his decision final, he didn't feel the excitement that he had thought he would feel.

The night after he officially became Dr. Benjamin Strickland, he and Julie went out on the town to celebrate. He had made reservations at one of the finer restaurants in Houston and had gone out and bought Julie a beautiful, blue silk dress for the occasion. He loved to see her in blue, as it made the blue in her eyes stand out, thus making them look even larger. He also bought her a bouquet of white roses. He surprised her by coming home around 4:00, with her gift and flowers. She was so excited, that she almost knocked him over, she hugged him so tight.

It truly was an evening of celebration. They had a bottle of champagne and Chateaubriand for two. There was a violinist that went from table to table playing during dinner. After dinner, he and Julie went to a local club and danced until the wee hours of the morning. He had the next week off and they had decided to not go anywhere this time but to just relax and enjoy each other. She had cancelled her student's lessons for that week and this was to be a chance to catch up on time missed over the last four years.

It was a wonderful week. They slept late every morning and spent time talking and dreaming about the future. Ben told Julie that he hoped within the next year that they could start looking for a house and move out of their little apartment. They talked about the kind of house they wanted and about the time they would be able to spend with each other, now that Ben had finished his residency.

One evening, as they lay side by side talking about these dreams, Julie brought up the subject of children again. She hadn't mentioned wanting to have a child in a long time, but Ben knew that the desire was still there and that she was just being patient and waiting for him to finish his residency before bringing up the subject anew. He wished that she had waited a while longer to talk about children because when she looked at him with those big, beautiful blue eyes, it was hard for him to refuse her anything. Besides, she hardly ever asked for anything and he knew how much she wanted a child. He lay there quietly for a few minutes and Julie wondered if she had picked the wrong time again to talk to him about her desire to be a mother.

After a while, Ben told her that he wanted children also but he thought it best to wait until they found a house and got it fixed up. Furthermore, he would like to have that next year just spending more time with each other, since the last four had been so consumed with his residency. He could see Julie's whole countenance drop and he quickly, without even thinking it through, promised her, that after the next year, they would start trying to have a child. She had brightened considerably at that because even though she would have preferred to start their family right away, a year was not very long and she could see Ben's point about having a house and spending more time together before having a child.

After that, they talked more about the kind of house they would start looking for and what area they wanted to live in. Ben could tell that her thoughts on a house were a bit different than his but finally agreed, that as long as it wasn't too far from his practice and her school, he would agree with most anything she wanted.

As that week ended, Ben felt that their relationship was closer than it had been in a long time. Julie's countenance had brightened and she once again seemed full of the joy and laughter that he had missed so much lately. Maybe she'd had it all along and he was just never there to enjoy it. He was excited also about their future. He even began to like the idea of a child a year or so down the road, especially if it made Julie this happy.

He was also excited about joining Dr. Williams' practice this next week. He was to move into the offices on Monday and start seeing patients by Tuesday. Ben wasn't quite sure what to expect, as he had spent the last four years seeing patients in a hospital and not an office environment.

Chapter 10

As Monday morning approached, he grew more and more excited. He was at the office a good half hour early that morning and had to wait outside in his car, as he didn't have a key yet. The first person to arrive was the office assistant/receptionist. He had met her once and she recognized him sitting in his car. Her name was Jeanette and she was in her early fifties. She was rather slim, had graying hair and from what he understood, pretty much ran the office and kept everyone, including the doctors in line. She waved to him and he followed her up the sidewalk to their building. After opening the door, she showed him around the offices. There were six patient rooms, Dr. Williams' office, Dr. Harvey's office, another office (which was to be his), a small lab, several restrooms, an office area for Jeanette and the billing clerk, Dorris, and the patient waiting area. As Jeanette finished showing him around, the nurses started to come in. He had met them once before. There were two RN's, Tammy and Charlotte and he would be hiring another nurse in the next few weeks.

After chatting with them for a few minutes, he went into his office and just sat for a minute at his desk. He and Julie had picked out and purchased office furniture the week before, during his time off, and it had already been delivered. He felt that the last eight long years had been worth it and here he was, finally ready to build his own patient base and start his practice.

He spent part of that day rearranging the furniture and moving his books and some other personal things in. He also interviewed five nurses and narrowed it down to two for Dr. Williams to interview as well. They had planned to come to a decision by the end of the next week and until then, Tammy or Charlotte would help assist him as he saw patients.

He spent time with both Dr. Williams and Dr. Harvey discussing the patient load and which patients would be shifted over to him. Dr. Williams explained that he worked in the abortion clinic two blocks away on Monday and Thursday mornings and took those afternoons off. He would be in the office on Tuesday, Wednesday and Friday. He did his hospital rounds late each afternoon. Dr. Harvey was usually in the office every morning during the week, as well as every afternoon, except Friday. He did his hospital round early each morning. They alternated on call at the hospital every other week. Dr. Harvey planned to shift some of his patient load over to Ben and start working at the abortion clinic on Tuesday mornings. Dr. Williams wanted to shift some of his also and spend one more morning a week at the abortion clinic.

Dr. Williams was the senior doctor in the practice and he suggested that Ben try to be there every day to begin with. The three of them would alternate weeks on call giving them more weekends free. Ben hadn't realized that Dr. Williams was gone two days a week from the clinic. He vaguely wondered why he wasn't given an afternoon off and wondered when the best time to do hospital rounds would be. However, he needed all the patients he could get as he had to increase his liability insurance now that he was in private practice and forty percent of his income from patients went back into the practice. That was better than the offer from Dr.

Johnson, at 50% of his patient income going back into the practice. Ben's first on call week would be the next week.

Ben was very excited as he went home that afternoon. He and Julie were actually able to sit down to dinner by 7:00, which was very unusual for them. He hardly let Julie get in a word edgewise that night, as he told her about the offices and about his work schedule. She could tell that he was so excited to begin seeing patients the next day and she was excited to finally have him home at nights except for those weeks he was on call.

The next morning, Ben was up bright and early. He went out for a jog and when he came back, he showered and shaved while Julie got their breakfast ready. As he shaved, he reflected that this was how he had wanted their lives to be from the very beginning, not rushing to the hospital at all hours of the night and morning. He thought about the wonderful dinner and evening he and Julie had together the night before. After breakfast, he left for the clinic and Julie left at the same time for school.

His patient load that day was heavier than he had expected, or maybe he just took longer with each patient than he should have. He felt that he needed to spend some time getting to know his patients and trying to make them as comfortable as possible with him. It took him a while to get use to the chart write up that the nurses had done. It was much different than the hospital charts. He ended up way behind the scheduled appointments and was still seeing patients at 6:30. This made Charlotte and Jeanette late leaving also. He didn't finally leave the office until after 7:30.

He called Julie right before leaving and she sounded upset. He had told her that morning that he should be home around 6:00 and hadn't taken the time to call her and tell her differently until now. She told him that she had prepared a special dinner for him, but that it probably wouldn't taste very good at this point. He was tired and irritable that he had gotten so far behind in seeing his patients so was rather short with Julie. He told her that he didn't want to talk about it on the phone and that he was leaving and would be home in about 15 minutes. He told her not to worry about dinner, if it wasn't any good, they could go out and eat. He sure hoped she would be in a better mood by the time he got home. All he wanted to do was eat and relax. He didn't need any hassles today.

He decided to stop on the way home and pick up their favorite Chinese takeout. Maybe that would cheer her up. However, that made him even later and it was around 8:15 when he finally arrived home. He heard Julie in the kitchen, so he put down his bag and briefcase and took the food into the kitchen. As he walked into the kitchen, he saw that Julie had set a special table with tablecloth and candles and that she had re-heated the dinner that she had prepared and it was on the table.

Her back was to him but when she heard him she turned around and started to say something. When she saw that he had Chinese food she burst into tears and ran into their bedroom, slamming the door. Ben wasn't sure what to do at that point. This was so unlike Julie. She was normally so calm and understanding.

At first he was surprised at her actions and then as he stood there he begin to get angry. After all, he only bought the Chinese to try and make up for being late and she had said their dinner was probably ruined. He put the Chinese food in the refrigerator and just sat at the kitchen table. Should he go in and try to calm her down or should he just go in the living room and turn on the TV and ignore her until she realized how silly she was acting? It had been such a busy day and all he wanted was to have a nice relaxing evening. As he sat there trying to decide whether he was at fault or Julie was, her sobs from the bedroom began to penetrate his heart. He didn't really feel he had done anything wrong but he hated to hear Julie crying, so he finally decided to see if he could comfort her in some way.

He quietly opened the door to their bedroom and found Julie lying facedown across the bed crying. He had seen her cry quietly for many reasons but he had never seen her sob like this. He went over and lay down beside her on the bed and just pulled her to him and held her. He wasn't sure what to say so he said nothing. He just hugged her and stroked her back and hair.

She finally quieted down and he asked her what he had done to make her cry like this. She had cried so hard that she could hardly talk but she finally was able to explain that she had fixed this special dinner to celebrate his first day of seeing patients in his own practice and how he said he would be home by 6:00 so she had planned the dinner around that time. She had fixed all his favorites, pork tenderloin on the grill, wild rice, asparagus and dinner rolls. She thought surely her would have called to tell her he was going to be late so she had started to worry about him. Then, when he did call he had sounded so gruff and short. But she said she had decided that it was okay, she would just warm up dinner again and make it a pleasant evening anyway because he had said he would be home in 15 minutes. Then 45 minutes later, in he walked with Chinese food and that was just the final straw to an already frustrating evening.

Ben still did not understand why she was so upset. He told her that she had said the dinner was probably ruined, so because he felt that it was his fault, he was just trying to help by getting the Chinese food and it took him longer to get it than he had expected. He also told her that his day had not gone as he had planned. His patient load was bigger than he had expected for the first day and then he must have spent too long with each patient because he got really behind and just didn't think to call. Instead, he was trying to finish as quickly as he could because he was causing Jeanette and Charlotte to have to work late also.

As he was explaining all this, tears began to stream down Julie's face again. Now he was totally confused. "What did I do now?" he asked. Julie replied, "You didn't do anything, I realize now that I overreacted and I'm sorry." She explained to him that when he was so late, it made her afraid that things would go back to being just like they had been during his residency and they would never have any time together. He pulled her to him again and held her close. He told her that he really believed they would have more time together. He explained that he just had to get used to the new routine and that he would try to get done quicker each day or at least if he saw that he would be late, he would be sure and call next time. He thanked her for her efforts to make this a special evening and to prepare his favorite meal. She thanked him for his thoughtfulness in getting the Chinese food. Ben pulled Julie up off the bed and gave her a long gentle kiss and said, "So we can save the Chinese for tomorrow and go eat that wonderful meal you worked so hard on!"

Dinner turned out to be special, even if it was a little late. Ben lit the candles and Julie served their plates. They talked and he told her more about his second day on the job. Now that she had calmed down, she listened with interest and was full of questions. Ben helped Julie do the dishes and then they went for a walk around the neighborhood. That gave them some more time to talk about their day and by the time they got back, they were both optimistic about the time they would have to spend together, now that Ben was part of a practice.

However, as the week progressed, Ben seemed to get more and more bogged down in seeing patients and working up the charts. He was hoping that after they hired an additional nurse, things would speed up a bit. Dr. Williams and Dr. Harvey managed to leave the office everyday before 5:00. However, he didn't seem to be able to get home before

7:00 or 8:00. It seemed as if they were shifting more and more patients over to him.

The next week, Karen, their new nurse, started but things didn't slow down for Ben. Because he was on call that week, he ended up spending several nights and most of the weekend at the hospital delivering babies.

A pattern of late nights at the office seemed to be developing. Ben would become absorbed in his work and he spent so much time with each patient, that he never left as early as the other two doctors. Then those weeks that he was on call seemed to come around all too often and most of them were spend at the hospital day and night.

As the weeks passed and there was no change in this hectic schedule, Julie never blew up at him again, the way she did that first night he was late for dinner. She just quietly withdrew into herself. He could tell by the music she played that her moods were not happy ones. Ben hated this but he didn't know what to do about it. He needed to see all the patients he could. His income was not what he had hoped it would be and he was trying to put as much money as possible in savings each week so that they could start looking at houses soon.

As he was driving home that night he began to think that maybe looking for a house was the solution. It might not be what he had hoped they could buy, but if they could find an older fixer upper for the right price, maybe they could go ahead and buy it and Julie could pour herself into fixing it up the way she wanted. That would solve two problems at once. It would take Julie's mind off him working late each night and get them out of that small apartment quicker.

When he arrived home that evening, Julie was in the den playing the piano. He just stopped by the door for a few minutes and listened to her play. It almost brought tears to his eyes. He could always hear Julie's emotions in her music and this was such a sad, lonely piece. He quietly went in and sat down beside her on the piano bench. She looked at him eye to eye when she had finished and smiled at him. He took her in his arms and hugged her tightly. Somehow, her smiles didn't light up her face anymore the way they used to.

He pulled back from her and took her hands in his. "Let's go out somewhere special to eat tonight," he prompted her. She asked him where and he told her that it would be a surprise. She hadn't fixed dinner because she wasn't sure when he would be home so they freshened up a bit and he took her to an Italian place in the city. It was owned by an Italian couple and the food was delicious. After they had been served their salads, Ben told Julie that he would like for them to start looking at houses that weekend. Julie told him that she thought he wanted to wait until they had more money saved. He explained to her his idea about trying to find a fixer upper and she began to share in his excitement. As they finished their salads and started on their entree', they excitedly discussed where they would start looking.

They decided they would look in the area they lived now. It was close to her school and his practice and she already had a base of private piano students established. Ben was not on call that week so they planned to spend all day Saturday looking at houses. They had a wonderful dinner that night. Julie was in better spirits than Ben had seen her in a long time. They talked about how much they could afford to spend on a house and what things they would look for. Ben's main concerns were cost and something that was structurally sound. Julie had completely different criteria. She wanted at least three bedrooms and two baths. She wanted something with lots of cabinet and closet space. Something with a living room and den, so that the piano could be in the living room and her lessons would not disturb Ben if he was home in the den. She wanted room for a study for him and a big back yard for their future children. They finished dinner and talked way into the night when they got home.

Saturday didn't seem to come soon enough for Ben or Julie. The rest of the week had been long for him, with his patient load seeming to increase daily. He wasn't able to get home before 8:00 any night that week. Julie had maintained her cheerful attitude however, because she was really looking forward to the weekend.

Julie was so excited about the possibility of buying a house, because in her mind, the sooner they were in a house, the sooner they could start trying to have their first child. She was sure that as they started a family, Ben would try to find more time to be at home.

Chapter 11

Ben and Julie both woke up early Saturday morning. Julie had set up an appointment to meet with a realtor around 9:30 and had told her exactly the kind of house they were looking for. They decided to go out for breakfast before meeting her so they left the apartment a little before 8:00. Julie was so excited that she could hardly eat. They ate a big breakfast thinking they would probably be looking at houses most of the day. Ben loved seeing the light back in Julie's eyes and the excitement in her voice.

They met the realtor, Sabrina Baker, at her office at exactly 9:30 and she visited with them for a while, getting to know them a little and talking to them about what she had been able to find for them to look at that day. She had set up appointments for them to see about ten different houses in their price range and in the area that Julie had specified.

The first eight houses they saw had some qualities that they liked but some that they didn't. Of course, most of them could be fixed up but several seemed to need a lot of structural repairs and Julie didn't like some of them because of lack of storage space or no yard. One was okay but the money needed to do what they would want to do was more than they would have after buying the house. They just weren't really excited about any that they had seen so far.

Ben could tell that Julie was beginning to get discouraged and he was just plain tired of looking. This house hunting was hard work. He had thought they would be able to get a lot more for what they were able to afford. Mrs. Baker told them not to get discouraged, because they still had two houses to look at and she had a feeling that they would especially like one of them.

She was right. The next house they looked at was in an older neighborhood and was located on a cul-de-sac. The street was lined with big oak trees and most of the yards had beautiful srubbery and flowers. The house they drove up to needed some yard work but it was a nice size in the front and had a huge back yard. Ben wasn't so sure about that because he didn't think he would have the time to maintain such a big yard. However, Julie assured him that she wanted to do all the yard work. The outside of the house was in need of paint, but looked structurally sound and the roof looked new.

Mrs. Baker told them that the people that owned the house had already done some renovating and that he had been transferred so they were selling before getting everything finished. Julie loved the outside and the neighborhood, but as soon as she entered the house, she knew that this was the one she wanted. The foyer had an old hardwood floor that looked as if it had been refinished. There were stairs to the right and a dining room to the left. You entered a big family room from the foyer and a formal living room was to the right of the stairs. The kitchen was big with an eat in area. It looked like it had been totally redone already, with lots of cabinet space. The flooring had been redone with clay brick colored tiles. The counter tops had recently been replaced and there were all new appliances. All that really needed to be done in the kitchen was to paint the cabinets. They were very big cabinets, typical of an older house and there were so many of them. Julie really loved the kitchen. There was a half bath downstairs.

Upstairs were four bedrooms and two baths. The master bedroom was really big and then there were three smaller bedrooms. One could be entered from the master bedroom so that one could be used for Ben's study and the other two were connected by the second bathroom. The bedrooms had large closets and high ceilings.

All of the rooms could use a fresh coat of paint. In fact Julie wanted to brighten up every room with color. The carpet was old but Julie was hoping there were hardwood floors underneath. If that was the case, she wanted to pull up the carpet and refinish the floors. She talked to Ben about all these possibilities as they walked through the house.

Mrs. Baker could tell that they really liked this one and hesitated before she told them that the selling price was $220,000, which was about $40,000 more than they had told her they could spend. Ben could see Julie's face fall as she heard the price. He could take or leave the house, although it was the nicest one they had looked at that day, but he knew from the moment they had walked in, that Julie had fallen in love with it. He told Mrs. Baker that $220,000 was just way out of their price range.

They went to look at the last house, but Julie had lost all of her enthusiasm. The last house was not one he would have wanted to sink money into anyway. As they went back to the real estate office, Mrs. Baker told them that she knew they really liked the house on Pelham Street and that maybe the owners would take a little less. She told them to go home and think about the most that they could afford to offer and let her know.

Julie was silent as they got in the car. Ben wanted so much to give her the house that she wanted, but he just didn't see how they could afford the payments on $220,000. He could put $20,000 down but that's what they had planned to put down on any house that they bought. That would still leave payments much higher than they could afford.

He asked Julie what she thought and she said that she knew they couldn't afford that much, but the house was just perfect. "Maybe we could offer them $195,000 and I could do most of the painting and wallpapering myself," she said hopefully. She told Ben that she would take on more private students to help pay for any remodeling. He told her that even then, he didn't think they could afford the monthly payments, but that he would work up some numbers and see what they could do. The more he talked to Julie, the more he wanted her to have that house.

She hardly talked about anything else that weekend. Ben could tell that no other house was going to measure up. On the way to the office Monday, he was still trying to figure out a way they could afford it. When he arrived in his office, he heard Dr. Williams walking down the hall to his office which was unusual. He was normally at the abortion clinic on Monday mornings. He followed him to his office to see what was going on. Dr. Williams told him that he just had to pick up some files before going to the clinic. He asked Ben about his weekend and normally Ben would have just said, "It was fine" and let it go at that, but he had been thinking about the house most of the morning so he told Dr. Williams about house hunting on Saturday and about how Julie had fallen in love with one of the houses, but that it was out of their price range.

Dr. Williams asked him to sit down for a minute. He told Ben that one of the doctors that worked several mornings at the abortion clinic was leaving and suggested that Ben work Wednesday or Friday mornings there. Ben wasn't so sure he wanted to do that after his experience during residency with performing abortions, but then Dr. Williams said that he could bring in an extra $1,000-$2,000 a month, just by working that one morning. Ben asked him wouldn't that affect their patient load at the clinic. He seemed to never get caught up as it was. Dr. Williams explained that with that extra income, he could afford to schedule fewer patients per day, which would in the long run give him more time at home and more money. "Why do you think I work there three mornings a week," asked Dr. Williams?

Ben told him that he would think about it and let him know. Dr. Williams said he needed to know by the end of the week as this doctor would be leaving then. Ben thanked him for telling him about the opportunity and then went back to his office to get ready for his first patient of the day.

He had a heavy schedule that day, but all through the day he kept thinking about what Dr. Williams had said and how that would make it possible to buy the house for Julie. He had not liked the few times that he had performed abortions at the hospital and he had no idea what the clinic was like but the money sounded almost too good to be true. If he could just be sure those nightmares about that first abortion wouldn't start again.

The more he thought about being able to get the house for Julie, the more he leaned toward telling Dr. Williams that he would work one morning a week at the clinic. "What would it hurt," he reasoned with himself. It was legal and it was much better for women to be able to come into a sterile, professional environment to get this procedure done, than the back alley doctors they used to use. He reasoned that it was in the best interest of the mother and the unwanted child. He really believed that no child should come into a world where it would be ignored or mistreated.

One other thought kept inserting itself among these rationalizations and that was that Julie would not approve. But it was for Julie and their future children that he would be doing this. If they wanted to eventually have children, they needed a bigger place. Besides, if he could make that kind of money one morning a week, then Dr. Williams was right, he could decrease his patient load each day and have more time to spend with Julie. Moreover, Julie worked during the day and never came to their offices anyway. She wouldn't have to know he was at the clinic instead of the office.

By the end of the day, he had convinced himself that this was the answer and that he would tell Dr. Williams first thing the next morning that he would like to take the doctors place that was leaving.

He went home in a great mood that night. Even though he got home a little late, he told himself that it wouldn't be too much longer and he would be making enough money to be home earlier each night with Julie. She was ecstatic when he told her that he had laid down some figures on paper and that he thought, if they were careful with their money, they might be able to afford the house. She hugged him hard enough to take his breath away. She was so happy, that she didn't even ask how they would be able to afford it. She just started planning what she would do with each room. Ben reminded her that they could not do all of that remodeling at once, only as they could afford it. However, nothing he said dampened Julie's spirits at that point.

She wanted to call the realtor that night, but he told her that he'd rather wait until tomorrow. What he didn't tell her was that he wanted to talk to Dr. Williams the next day and make sure he would be able to work at the clinic before calling and making an offer on the house. Even though Julie didn't understand why Ben hesitated in calling Mrs. Baker, she was satisfied just knowing that they were going to try to buy the house. All that night she dreamed of how she wanted each room to eventually look.

The next morning Ben went in a little early to have a chance to talk with Dr. Williams. He told him that he would like to work at least one morning a week at the abortion clinic. He asked Dr. Williams if he had spoken with any other physicians about filling the position. Dr. Williams told him that he had waited to see if Ben wanted Friday mornings before looking for another doctor. He was excited that Ben had decided to join he and Dr. Harvey at the clinic. He told Ben to get Jeanette to reschedule his appointments for next Friday and he could start then. Ben asked if he could visit the clinic one day that week just to become familiar with things before starting the next week. Dr. Williams told him that if he could reschedule a few of his appointments tomorrow morning he could go over to the clinic with him then.

Ben put in a call to Mrs. Baker before his first patient arrived. He told her that they would like to make an offer on the house on Pelham Street. They wanted to offer $195,000. She told him that she would draw up an offer and bring it by that evening for he and Julie to sign. She felt reasonably sure that they would accept the offer because they would be moving at the end of the month and were anxious to sell. The rest of that day was so busy for Ben that it flew by. He was able to get home by 6:30 that evening and he quickly told Julie that he had called the realtor and that she would be by at 7:30 for them to sign the offer.

Julie had dinner ready, so they sat down to eat before Mrs. Baker came, but she was so excited that she could hardly eat. Ben was soon caught up in her enthusiasm and they planned what they wanted to do to the house, as they were able to afford it. He reminded her that he would not have a lot of time to help decorate, but Julie seemed to be excited about it regardless.

Mrs. Baker was there promptly at 7:30. It didn't take Ben very long to read over the papers and then he and Julie signed them. He asked Mrs. Baker what the next step was and she explained that she would present the offer to the owners and if they accepted, then they would have to go through loan approval. That should take about 4 weeks and assuming their loan was approved, they could move in by late July.

After Mrs. Baker left, Julie hugged Ben tightly and told him that she didn't know how he worked it out financially but it must be right, because the timing was so perfect. They would be able to move in before school started back in September. As he held her and saw how happy she was, he pushed the thought of working at the abortion clinic to the back of his mind. What mattered most to him was that he could make Julie this happy.

He warned her not to get too excited until their offer was accepted. After all they did offer $25,000 less than the asking price. That calmed Julie down a little but she was the eternal optimist and told he that she just knew that it was meant to be their house, so she wasn't even worried about it not being accepted.

Chapter 12

The next morning, Karen had rearranged Ben's appointments so that he had the morning free. He had arrived at the office early to get some things done before Dr. Williams arrived to take him to the abortion clinic, so he was there about an hour when Dr. Williams tapped on his office door. When they arrived at the clinic, they drove around to the back parking lot, but they had to drive past the front of the building first. Ben was amazed to see a group of people out in front of the clinic with signs that read "Save the Children" and "Its not tissue, it's a baby". Most of the people were women but there were also several clergy there. Ben had seen this type of thing on the News but it really shocked him to actually see these people in front of the place he would be working each week.

Dr. Williams just seemed to be ignoring them, so Ben asked him what was going on. He told Ben that he hardly even noticed these people any more. There always seemed to be at least a few of them picketing each day. Ben wasn't so sure he would be able to ignore them but at least they would be going in the back entrance, so they wouldn't have to walk through them to get into the clinic.

Dr. Williams introduced Ben to Glenda the receptionist and to Barbara and Sharon the nurses. He then showed Ben around the clinic. There were four rooms with equipment set up, to perform the abortions and two recovery rooms. There was such a stark difference between these rooms and the delivery rooms at the hospital. Ben was used to delivery rooms with warm colored wall paper, several chairs and a television. The labor and delivery rooms were one and the same at the hospital. These rooms were so white and stark looking. There were two restrooms and the waiting area. It was actually larger than Ben had thought it would be and very clean and sanitary. This reaffirmed his rationalization that it was better for the women to come here, rather than going to some hole in the wall place to have their abortions, as they used to have to do before abortion became legal.

Dr. Williams had brought Ben over early before any patients arrived, so that he could better show him around, but as they were finishing their tour Ben heard noise in the waiting area signifying that their morning was about to begin. He wasn't actually performing abortions that day. He was just there to get a feel for what he would be doing Friday morning.

As the nurse brought back the first patient, Ben was shocked to see that this wasn't a woman at all but a young girl in her teens. She didn't look to be more than fifteen or sixteen at the most. She seemed very frightened and unsure of herself. The nurse prepped her and then Dr. Williams came into the room to start the procedure. He had thought that Dr. Williams would talk with her a while first and try to reassure her, but he barely talked to her at all while he very quickly began the procedure.

Ben could see the young girl's hands trembling and a single tear ran down her cheek, as the fetus within her was aborted. He wanted to go over and hold her hand and try to comfort her but he caught himself and reminded himself that this was Dr. Williams' patient. He was only here to observe. Still, it bothered him. Not as much as that first abortion had because the fetus was not as far along and he had convinced himself that it wasn't a baby until after a certain point in development. The age of the young girl and how emotional she seemed to be bothered him more than the abortion itself. Both Dr. Williams and the nurse seemed to treat her with no warmth at all. After the procedure, the nurse wheeled the young girl in to the adjoining recovery room and he went with Dr. Williams to scrub and prepare for the next patient.

The rest of that morning went much the same. Dr. Williams did a total of ten abortions that morning. To Ben's amazement, all but three of them were teenage girls. It was such a fast paced morning that he didn't have a chance to ask Dr. Williams about this until they had finished and were on the way back to their offices.

As they were driving back Ben commented on how surprised he had been at the ages of the patients that had come in that morning for abortions. Dr. Williams told him that they worked in conjunction with several high schools in the area and that he would find that a lot of their patients were high school girls. "What do their parents say," asked Ben? "Don't they want to be there with their daughters?" Dr. Williams explained that most of the parents didn't even know their daughters were pregnant. They go to the school counselor or nurse and they advice them of their options, one of which is our clinic. If the girl decides to have an abortion, the nurse or counselor writes them an excused absence from classes and then a bus brings them to the clinic and takes them back to school. When they get back to school, they usually rest in the nurses office and then return to class when they feel up to it or go home after school the same as any other day.

Ben couldn't believe what he was hearing. He had thought that their patients would be consenting adults who had some very good reason for not wanting to have a child. He hadn't like the thought of working at the clinic before but now he didn't know if he could do this even one morning a week. He expressed these feelings to Dr. Williams who laughed and said, "Ben, it is perfectly legal and these girls are too young to be mothers. It's the best thing for them. We help them to continue with their high school years and not ruin their lives by having a child they are in no way prepared to have, but if you no longer want the job, I know another doctor at the hospital that asked me about the opening."

Ben thought about it and was tempted to tell Dr. Williams to give it to the other doctor, but then he remembered Julie and the house that they had made an offer on. He began to reason with himself that Dr. Williams was right. It was the best thing for these girls. He told Dr. Williams that he still wanted to work at the clinic and that he would be ready to start on Friday. Dr. Williams slapped him on the back and told him that he was glad about his decision. He shared that he had been hesitant at first also but that it was a good way to make some extra money and perform a service that was well needed.

That Friday was not easy for Ben. He performed six abortions that day and all but two of them were on high school girls. As the weeks passed, it became easier and easier however. It eased his conscious a lot, when he would go home and share in Julie's excitement about their house. Their offer had been accepted and they were scheduled to move in four weeks.

Chapter 13

Ben's weeks grew increasingly busy. Initially, he had cut back his patient load, as he was spending two instead of one morning a week at the clinic. Dr. Williams had not been able to find another doctor for the other morning available so Ben had agreed to work that morning also. However, as the weeks went by his patient load began to pick up again. He felt bad because he was so seldom home. Julie had to do most of the work on the house. He helped her whenever he could, on the weekends that he wasn't on call and some at night, if he didn't get home too late. However, Julie never complained. She seemed so much happier, now that she was involved in fixing up their new home. She had repainted every room. He had to admit that the house was beautiful and that along with her musical ability, Julie had an eye for decorating. Each night, when he did get home, she was excited to show him some other little thing that she had done or bought for the house.

Never once, did Julie question where the extra money in their account was coming from. Ben still felt guilty at times about not telling her he was working at the abortion clinic. He had always felt that honesty in a relationship was very important, but somewhere in his heart he knew she would be upset about him performing abortions. She never called him at the office anyway. She always paged him, so that he could call her back when he was free.

As the house began to take shape and Julie again had more free time on her hands, she decided to broach the subject of children with Ben. She wanted a baby so much that sometimes she ached inside for a child. Ben was suppose to be off that weekend, so she decided that she would make a special candlelight dinner for Friday night and bring up the subject of children. After all, they seemed to be doing better financially and now they had a house big enough for children.

Ben had felt bad about the lack of time he was able to give Julie lately, so he tried very hard, that Friday, to get through with his patients early and be home by 6:30. Julie had mentioned that she had planned something special. It turned out to be an easy afternoon and he was able to get home by 6:00. When he walked in the door, he was drawn to the kitchen by the wonderful smells coming from that part of the house. Julie was surprised to see him so early and dropped what she was doing to give him a big hug and kiss. She told him to go upstairs and change into something more comfortable, that dinner would be ready in about thirty minutes.

He loved it when Julie was in one of her "surprise" moods. He went to their bedroom and decided to take a shower before changing. After his shower, he put on some jeans and a sweatshirt and went back to the kitchen, to find dinner was ready. Julie had set up the dining room with table cloth and candles. They hardly ever ate in the dining room, since it was just the two of them. Most of the time, they either ate in the kitchen or took their dinners in the den and ate on TV trays while watching TV or a movie.

Ben was beginning to wonder what the special occasion was. Julie had prepared Chicken Cordon Bleu and rice and asparagus. She had made homemade rolls and an apple pie for dessert. Ben finally couldn't stand it any longer and asked "What's going on? Are we celebrating something?" "We'll talk about that later," Julie said, "Let's just enjoy our dinner now." And enjoy it he did. It was the first time in a few weeks he had eaten dinner before 8:00 or 9:00.

Julie talked about some of her more interesting students and asked him how things were going with his patients. He almost started talking about the clinic but caught himself just in time. He tried to steer the subject away from his work and they began to talk about Julie's family and all that was happening with her brothers and sister. They finished their meal and did the dishes together. Then they went into the den, where Julie had started a fire, to relax and have a glass of wine.

Julie told him that she had talked with her parents that afternoon and they were thrilled with their invitation to visit them for Christmas. In fact, they had worked it out so that her whole family would come and spend Christmas with them this year. Ben was as excited as Julie, since it had been so long since they had seen her parents.

As they were discussing some of the things they wanted to do and show them, Julie snuggled up close to Ben and said, "Wouldn't it be great if we could tell my parents at Christmas, that they were going to be grandparents?" Ben laughed and hugged her, telling her that now he understood what all the special treatment that night had been about. Then he got more serious and told Julie that he knew how much she wanted a child and how patient she had been in the years since they were married. She was a little disappointed and asked him didn't he want to have a child as much as she did. He decided to be perfectly honest with her and explained that at times, he was really nervous about being a father because his childhood had not been a happy one. He also told her that he didn't want to have an only child so when they started a family he wanted to have at least two and that their lives would be changed forever.

She hugged him close and told him that she knew he would be a great father and that it would be a good change.

As they talked, he began to pick up on her enthusiasm. "Well, Mrs. Strickland, I suppose we should start working on this new addition to our family tonight," Ben said, as he took Julie into his arms. That was the most wonderful night of sharing and loving that Ben could ever remember them having.

He had never seen Julie happier. Each day she just bubbled with enthusiasm. She was anxious to start fixing up one of the rooms as a nursery, but decided to wait until after Christmas because they needed the room when her family visited. He thought she was jumping the gun a little, as she wasn't even pregnant yet. He did enjoy seeing her this happy, however.

Thanksgiving was there before they knew it that year. They were so busy with the house and each of their jobs, that time seemed to fly by. Julie had suggested that they spend Thanksgiving with his parents since they would be with hers for Christmas but he was silently thankful that he had to tell her they couldn't because he would be on call over Thanksgiving.

This disappointed her a little but nothing could bring down her spirits for long because she had bought and done a home pregnancy test the day before and it was positive. She was waiting until Thanksgiving Day to tell Ben. Then they would truly have something special to be thankful for.

They planned to spend Thanksgiving at home, just the two of them. Julie cooked a small turkey and made stuffing, green beans, sweet potato casserole, mashed potatoes and pumpkin pie for dessert. It was a quiet but wonderful day and even though Ben was on call, he only had to go into the hospital once, early that morning. They planned to have dinner around 4:00 that afternoon.

When Ben got back from the hospital around 11:00, Julie already had the turkey in the oven and was in the process of making the pumpkin pie. He helped her for a while in the kitchen. He snapped the green beans and cut up the potatoes for the mashed potatoes. He wasn't much of a cook but he loved watching Julie in the kitchen. She did seem a little pale to him though.

He was carrying on his end of the conversation while peeling potatoes, when he looked up to see Julie run from the kitchen, into the bathroom to be sick. He quickly got her a cold rag and wiped her forehead. After she seemed to have finished throwing up, he helped her to the couch and sat down beside her. He thought she must have one of the stomach viruses that had been going around lately. He told her to just lie there and not worry about finishing dinner. She probably didn't need to be eating anyway. She assured him that she was okay now and that she fully intended to get up and finish their Thanksgiving meal. He tried to convince her that if she had a virus, she needed to rest and not put anything in her stomach.

Julie sat up and smiled weakly. Taking his hand, she told him that she had wanted to wait until their meal that afternoon to tell him, but it wasn't because of a virus that she had been sick. It was because she was carrying their child. Ben didn't know what to say. It took a minute for what Julie had said to sink in. He just held her hand and stared at her with his mouth open. She was beginning to worry about his reaction, when he snapped out of it and sat next her on the sofa pulling her into his arms. "Oh Julie," he said, tears streaming down his face, "I know we've been trying but I've been so busy, I had no idea!"

"Are you happy," she asked? At this point she was crying too. "Happy, I'm ecstatic." laughed Ben! "I can't believe we're really having a baby." They sat on the couch just hugging and laughing and crying all at the same time. Then Ben took her by the shoulders and looked her in the eyes asking her if she was sure she felt okay. Julie told him that she felt fine now. In fact, that was the first time she had been sick. Ben asked her when she found out and she told him that she had done a home pregnancy test two days before. She explained that she had wanted to wait and tell him during their Thanksgiving meal as a surprise. He assured her that not only was he very surprised, but also very excited.

Ben made Julie lie back down on the couch while he finished their dinner, much to her protest. Julie knew Ben hardly ever cooked but was amazed at what a wonderful job he did on the rest of their meal. She was feeling fine again by the time dinner was done and they sat down for dinner with true reason to be happy and thankful.

Chapter 14

Julie had asked Ben, during dinner on Thanksgiving, if she should call and make an appointment at his office. Ben referred her to another Obstetrician that he knew from the hospital. He told her that it would probably be better to use someone outside their offices. Julie didn't completely understand his reasoning but had agreed and had made an appointment for the following week.

In truth, Ben just didn't want Julie coming to their offices because, even though he wouldn't be her doctor, she might come at a time when he was at the clinic and he didn't want her to find out about him working there, especially now. In fact, that week performing the abortions bothered him in a way that it hadn't for a long time. He guessed it was just knowing that, in seven months, he and Julie would be having a baby. However, he was making more money than he could ever hope to make in private practice, at least for the next five to six years. Besides, working at the clinic had allowed him a little more free time at home. He really needed the extra money and wanted the extra time, now that Julie was pregnant.

Julie did stop by his office on the way home from her appointment with Dr. Beck. Ben was just glad it wasn't one of his clinic days. After seeing his last patient, he went back to his office to find Julie waiting there for him. She was so excited. She told him that she was about seven weeks pregnant and that the baby was due sometime around the end of July. He asked her what the doctor had said and she told him that she was very healthy and the baby seemed fine. They had done some blood work and she had an appointment to come back in a month.

Ben gave Julie a big hug and told her that he had just finished with his last patient so they could leave together and go out to eat to celebrate. She hadn't had any more problems, so far, with nausea and she was starving, so she eagerly agreed. They went to their favorite Italian restaurant. Julie could not stop talking about the baby. He had never seen her so excited. He had also never seen her eat so much. She wondered if it would be a boy or girl. She hoped for a boy but he hoped for a girl. They discussed whether they wanted to know the sex ahead of time and decided they both wanted to wait until the baby was born. They talked about which room to make into a nursery after Christmas and how excited they were to tell Julie's parents.

Julie wanted to call and tell his parents that evening but for some reason he kept putting her off. He convinced her to wait until that weekend. They were so involved with excitement and talk that they barely noticed what they were eating. Ben reminded Julie that this would be their last Christmas together without children. Julie told him that they would make it very special for each other because once children came along, they were the main focus at Christmas. Ben wasn't so sure about that. He didn't remember being the center of attention at Christmas when he was growing up. He told her that most of the time his parents had been out of town and he had been left at home with their housekeeper. Julie couldn't imagine that and assured him that it wouldn't be that way in their home, especially since they didn't have any hired help.

They went home as soon as they had finished dinner and Julie decided to go to bed even thought it was early. She told

Ben that she felt so tired lately. He assured her that what she was feeling was normal and that she should try and get plenty of rest during the next eight months.

After Julie went to bed, Ben turned the TV on but he couldn't concentrate on what he was watching. He kept thinking of what it would be like to be a father. Sometimes he was so excited but then at other times he was just scared. He wanted so much to be a good father. He wanted to have the time to spend with his children that his parents had never had. Even though performing abortions seemed to bother him again these days, he found himself wondering if he might be able to work another half day at the clinic and cut down his patient load at the office even more. He wanted to be with Julie as much as he could before the baby came. Besides, they would need even more money once they had children.

The time seemed to fly by between Thanksgiving and Christmas. Ben was worried that Julie was trying to do too much. She wanted their house to be perfect, before her family came and she had her Christmas music program at the school to prepare for. That meant extra rehearsals during the middle of December. He had been able to be at most of her programs over the last few years and knew that she went all out with the students. She seemed to be doing fine, however. He was amazed at how energetic she seemed, especially since she had seemed so tired just the week before.

He helped as much as he could with household chores, when he wasn't seeing patients or on call. He had managed to get out of being on call Christmas even though he was the junior doctor in their practice. He had also worked it so he could be at the abortion clinic one more morning a week after the holidays.

He wanted this Christmas to be special for them. Sometimes, he felt excited about being a parent but other times he wished things could stay just the way they were with just he and Julie. He just wasn't sure he would like being a father. He liked the way things were now. He could never share these feelings with Julie because it would crush her. She had wanted children ever since they were married. He knew she would be a wonderful mother but he wasn't so sure he would be a very good father. Regardless, he soon would be and he wanted this Christmas to be the best they had ever had.

He was really glad Julie's family was coming but she seemed so busy and he wanted her to slow down and enjoy their time together. He certainly couldn't say that to her because he was the one who had been so busy all their married life, not her. Sometimes, he wished he had chosen another profession that was less demanding, but deep down he knew he wouldn't be happy being anything other than a doctor.

Ben shook himself. He didn't know why he found himself in these reflective moods so much lately. He had seemed to be that way since they talked with his parents, the past weekend. They had seemed so excited about the baby, but he just couldn't make himself believe they were sincere. They could sound excited over the phone but would they ever make the time to see the baby or spend any time with them, once the baby was born? It saddened him that he hardly ever missed his parents the way Julie seemed to miss her family. He didn't want his child to ever feel that way about him.

It was only a week until Christmas. Julie's last day at school before the holidays was Friday and then her parents would come the following Wednesday. He was on call that weekend and hoped that he didn't get called into the hospital too often because he wanted to help her with the last minute shopping and cleaning. They still had to buy their tree and decorate it. They had put off decorating until after Julie's program at school was over because extra practices took up so much of her time. As usual, her program was wonderful. The students loved to perform for Julie. She always found a way to bring out the best in them. Julie loved her students and because they knew that, even the not so talented ones made every effort to do well for her.

They had planned to get their tree that Friday evening, after he got home from the office and Julie was finished with her teaching for the holidays. However, Julie seemed so tired, that Ben told her to rest on the couch and he would go get Chinese and bring it back for dinner. She gladly agreed and when he got back she was fast asleep on the couch. She looked so sweet and peaceful that Ben hated to awaken her. As he stood there debating whether to wake her up or let her sleep for another hour, she must have felt him looking at her because she woke up with a start. She couldn't believe she had fallen asleep. Ben asked her if she felt like eating or just wanted to go to bed and she said, "Are you kidding, I'm famished!" She seemed to wake up refreshed and they had a wonderful meal and watched a Christmas movie that he had rented. It was so warm and cozy in their house and they were both so relaxed, that they decided to wait until morning to get the tree and bring down the decorations from the attic.

The next morning, they woke up bright and early, full of energy and eager to start the day. They ate some breakfast and then worked together to clean the house before going to get the tree. They were just about to head out to do some shopping, get a few groceries and get their tree when Ben was beeped and had to go to the hospital. Julie tried not to seem disappointed but she knew by this time, that there was no way to know how long Ben would be gone. She told him to help her get the boxes of decorations down and she would be decorating the rest of the house while he was gone. Then, when he returned they could go find a tree.

It was late afternoon before Ben was able to leave the hospital and return home. The house looked beautiful. Julie had decorated the windows with greenery and candles and had wrapped greenery and lights around the banister of the stairs. She had put a big wreath over the fireplace and had candles and greenery on the mantle. She had other decorations throughout the house making it look merry and festive.

Ben loved how warm and homey she made everything look. While decorating their house, she had chosen colors and furniture that made you feel relaxed and at home. It looked beautiful but not untouchable like his house had seemed to him. Now it looked even more that way with everything decorated. The only thing missing was the tree. They decided to go out to dinner and get the tree and then save the shopping until the next day so they could come home that night and decorate the tree.

They chose a huge blue spruce that was perfectly shaped. In their little apartment they had always had a small tree, but this year, they had plenty of room and Julie wanted something big and beautiful. Ben was afraid that when they got it in the house it might be too big but, after trimming a little off the bottom, it fit perfectly. However, it did look a lot bigger in the house than at the tree lot. They had bought a few more decorations while they were out and two more strands of lights. He hoped it would be enough. He set up the tree and put on the lights, while Julie organized the decorations. They took their time and laughed and reminisced, thoroughly enjoying every minute of it. Julie had made Christmas cookies earlier in the day while she waited for him to return from the hospital. He built a fire in the fireplace and they had coffee and cookies while listening to Christmas music and admiring their tree.

The next morning, Ben had a call from the hospital early but was back home by 10:30. Julie had slept late and then fixed a big breakfast. He had called her from the hospital before he left to come home, so it was ready when he got there. They ate a leisurely breakfast and then left to do some Christmas shopping. They shopped for each of her family members and for his mother and father. Everytime they passed baby clothes, Julie wanted to stop and look. He had to admit they were cute.

They stopped for lunch about 2:00 and then decided to separate for a while and shop for each other. It took Ben a while but he finally found the perfect gift for Julie. He bought her a fourteen karat gold slide bracelet with an ornate piece with his birthstone in it and one with hers. He thought she would like this as he could get her one for each child they had and any other special occasion that came along. He also bought her a book that she had been wanting to read and some of her favorite perfume. He had it all wrapped and was finished in time to meet her at the place they had designated.

She wasn't there when he got there, so he went to the food court to get a coke. It had taken Julie a little longer to find what she wanted for Ben. She had gotten him several compact discs that he liked and a book but the special thing that she got him was a video camera. They had talked before about getting one but now that they were going to have a baby, she especially wanted to have it. It was really a present for both of them but she had saved some of her money that she earned from private piano lessons and gotten the really expensive one that Ben wanted. He was there waiting for her when she finally finished.

Julie loved shopping and it had been a wonderful afternoon together. However, she was a lot more tired than she had realized. When they finally sat down in the car, it was all she could do to hold her eyes open. Ben was beeped on the way home, so they drove through McDonalds and got a burger, fries and shake before he dropped her at home and went to the hospital. Julie ate her dinner, kicked off her shoes and turned the TV on. She was asleep in ten minutes and didn't wake up until Ben got home around midnight.

Julie spent the early part of the week getting all the presents wrapped and under the tree and doing some baking and cleaning for Christmas. Her parents, David, Carl and Stephanie were flying in on Thursday, Christmas Eve. Their plane was due to arrive at 10:30 that morning. Tommy and Ashley's flight would arrive at 10:00.

Ben had taken Thursday, Friday, Saturday and Sunday off. He hadn't had any time off since joining the practice except a few days to move into their house, so he was really looking forward to it. The closer Thursday got, the more excited Julie was. Ben didn't think she could clean one more thing in the house. Everything was spotless in his opinion. However, Julie woke up early Thursday morning to get a few more little things done. They had an early breakfast and left about 9:00 for the airport.

Tommy and Ashley's flight was about 30 minutes late, so they only arrived 5 minutes before the rest of the family. Ben and Julie were waiting at baggage claim for them. Shortly after they had retrieved their bags Julie saw David walking towards them. He had grown so tall since they had last seen him. He ran up to Julie and grabbed her in a big hug. It didn't seem possible that David was fifteen. He let go of Julie and hugged Ben. Then the rest of the family walked up. Carl was out of college for the holidays and had been able to come. Stephanie had brought her boyfriend, Peter, and last but not least Mr. and Mrs. Bennett stepped up for their hugs.

They made quite a scene, as there were so many of them and they were all hugging and crying. They finally moved to the side and as usual, everyone was talking at once. This was the first time they had met Peter, but Stephanie had written Julie all about him. They were both Freshman at the local junior college. They finally all headed toward baggage claim to get their bags and David took Mr. Bennett to the rental car area to rent a van while they were there. There was no way to fit everyone plus their luggage in Ben and Julie's two small cars. It took them almost an hour to get out of the airport and head toward home. Mr. and Mrs. Bennett rode with them and Tommy drove the van with everyone else. Ben could tell that it was going to be an exciting Christmas.

Since they only had three bedrooms, Julie had taken some time before they came figuring out where everyone would sleep. She put her parents in one of the bedrooms, Tommy and Ashley in the other one and she had put a roll away bed in the study for Stephanie. Carl and David were on the sofa bed and she had rented another roll away bed for Peter, in the living room. Their house had seemed large enough to Ben but all of a sudden, it was shrinking before his eyes. There seemed to be wall to wall beds, luggage and people.

Julie had brought everyone in, to show them around the house, before bringing in all the presents and luggage. Everyone loved their new home and exclaimed over all the decorating they had done. Finally, everyone was settled in and Julie and her mother and sister went to the kitchen to start their meal. They had decided to eat early, since none of them had eaten lunch. Julie had made a big pot of homemade soup that morning, so she heated it up and they had soup and sandwiches.

It was a lively meal, with everyone sharing what was going on in their lives. Tommy loved the Air Force. He and Ashley were currently stationed in Rome, New York. He talked to them about his assignment there and Ashley told them about her job at a local bank in Rome. They were happy to leave behind all that snow to come and enjoy the sunshine in Texas.

Carl was in his Senior year at the University of Illinois. He was studying to be a marine biologist. They tried to probe into his social life but he told them he didn't date just one girl. He had several that he enjoyed going out with. Ben and Julie looked at each other and smiled. Carl was the brainy one of the family but he was also very handsome.

Stephanie was in her first year of college and studying Elementary Education. She and Peter could not keep their eyes off each other. At first, Julie thought she was too young to be so serious but then she remembered that she had met and fallen in love with Ben when she was a Freshman. Besides, Stephanie had started college a year after graduating. She had worked for a year first.

David was his usual boisterous self. He was beginning to mature but would probably never loose that mischievous nature of his. He had a comment about everything and everyone and kept them all laughing. Mr. and Mrs. Bennett were rather quiet during the meal. They just seemed to sit back and enjoy having everyone together again.

After their meal, David wanted them all to pick a present to open. They convinced him to wait until they had cleared the table and done the dishes, but that was as long as they could hold him off, so they gathered in the den around the Christmas tree. As was the tradition, everyone picked one present from under the tree and then each took turns opening them.

Ben opened a new sweater from Mr. and Mrs. Bennett. Julie opened a wallet from David. Tommy opened a book and Ashley a new scarf. Carl's present was some new cologne; David got a compac disc that he wanted, Stephanie opened her present from Peter which was a beautiful heart shaped necklace and his from her was a picture that she'd had made and framed for him.

Mr. and Mrs. Bennett opened theirs last. They had picked a joint gift from Ben and Julie to open. Julie was so excited as they were opening it that she could hardly sit still. She reached over and squeezed Ben's hand. They had gotten them a large photo album with "We Are Proud Grandparents" on the cover. They opened the box and both looked at each other and then at Ben and Julie. Julie couldn't stand it any longer. She jumped up and ran over and hugged her mom and dad saying, "This is for when you become grandparents in July!"

Everyone began talking and hugging at once. The presents were forgotten for a while, as everyone wanted to know all the details. When was it due? Did Julie feel okay? How long had they known? It was midnight before they got all the clutter cleaned up and had calmed down enough for everyone to even think about sleep.

As Julie snuggled down next to Ben in the bed, she sighed and told him that she could never remember being any happier than she was at that moment. They both were exhausted but it had been a wonderful day.

Julie had planned to get up by 6:30 and get some things done in the kitchen before everyone woke up, but she overslept. She was so exhausted from the excitement of the day before. She didn't wake up until 8:00 and when she did, Ben was already up and had started breakfast. Tommy and her dad were also in the kitchen. They told her just to go relax and they would do breakfast. She gladly went back to their bedroom and took a shower and dressed. By the time she was finished, breakfast was ready and the rest of the family was up and about.

The men had prepared a wonderful breakfast of hash browns, sausage, scrambled eggs and toast. Everyone seemed famished and ate until everything was gone. The women cleaned the dishes since the men had cooked and then they all gathered around the tree again to finish opening the mound of presents that waited for them. It took them the rest of the morning to open presents. Everyone had to see everyone else open theirs and then gather up all the paper and gifts and each find somewhere to put theirs. It was a morning filled with love and laughter.

After they had finished opening presents, which took a good two hours, Julie went to the kitchen to start Christmas dinner. She had put the turkey in that morning, before they started opening presents, and had made the pies and cake the day before her family came. Her mother, Stephanie and Ashley all pitched in and helped and they had the rest of the meal ready in no time. They were ready to eat by 3:00. They had so much food, that Julie decided to serve it buffet style from the sideboard. They ate and talked until they couldn't hold anymore.

They were all so tired and full after dinner, that they could hardly move from the table. Mr. and Mrs. Bennett insisted that they clean up after the meal, so the rest of them decided to take a walk. It was a beautiful day and the weather was so much milder than in Chicago and New York, that all they needed was a light jacket. They looked like a small army walking through the neighborhood and probably sounded like one with all the noise they made. When they returned an hour later, the kitchen was clean and Mr. and Mrs. Bennett had left a note saying that they were taking a nap. That sounded good to Julie but she hated to miss any of the fun. Ben finally convinced her to rest at least for an hour and he would wake her before they had any "fun".

They all lazed around the rest of the day, watching TV and played some games that night. They decided that they were so full from dinner, that everyone could just fend for themselves that night and make a sandwich if they were hungry. It was a wonderful Christmas and none of them got to bed before midnight again.

When they were finally in their room alone, Julie told Ben how much she loved the bracelet he gave her. He told her that he would give her a piece for each child and other special occasions. Then all of a sudden she started crying. Ben thought he had done something wrong, but she assured him that it was just happy and tired tears. He made her promise to take it easier the rest of the week.

However, taking it easy was not in the picture. They had a great week with her family but things were always busy and hectic. They took them to the airport Sunday evening. Everyone had seemed to have a wonderful time, even Peter seemed to fit into the family and enjoy himself. Julie was in tears as she told everyone goodbye. Her mother promised that she and Mr. Bennett would be back in July when the baby came and that seemed to console Julie a little. However, she cried all the way home. Ben had gotten used to Julie's emotions whenever she left her family. He would miss them too but he was actually glad to get their home quieter and back to normal. He never told Julie that, however, he just held her and let her get all her crying out.

Chapter 15

B en was actually glad to go back to work. He loved his work at the OB/GYN clinic. He loved the deliveries at the hospital. He really didn't like the days at the abortion clinic but they were a way for him to have the extra income that he needed and he had actually convinced himself that he was performing a much needed service. Julie had seemed anxious to get back to work that morning also. She still seemed a little sad but her spirits never stayed down for very long. He knew that as soon as she got busy with her students again she would be fine.

His week was very busy and so was Julie's. By the end of the week, it seemed like they had never had the days off. They had planned to buy the paint and start on the nursery that weekend but both were so tired they decided to just rest. It was a much needed quiet weekend. Julie had been having a bout with morning sickness again that week and she spent a lot of time in bed. She continued to have a problem with it the rest of January and Ben was beginning to worry about her because she was actually loosing weight instead of gaining.

By February, Julie was back to her normal self and seemed to have gotten over her nausea. At her February visit to the doctor, she had gained one pound and the baby seemed fine. They spent a lot of the winter months working on the baby's room. They painted it a light yellow and Julie stenciled pastel colored balloons around the top of the walls. They found a throw rug with all of the pastel colors in it to go in front of the crib. Julie was working on several cross stitch patterns with animals and balloons.

When Spring finally came, Ben and Julie went to garage sales on the weekends he wasn't on call and found the baby a bed, a dresser, a changer and an old wooden high chair. They sanded and refinished the furniture a light oak color. Ben was really beginning to look forward to this baby. It helped that Julie kept him so involved in everything they did to the nursery. They had so much fun decorating, refinishing and shopping for things, and as the room began to look ready for a baby, he and Julie both would go in and just stand there quietly, wondering what it would be like when the newest little Strickland came into their lives.

Julie would be through teaching for the summer by June 10th. The baby wasn't due until July 14th. Ben knew they shouldn't travel too far but he wanted them to take a week's vacation before the baby came. It would be their last chance to get away, just the two of them, for a while. He couldn't get a doctor to cover his patients and the clinic for him until the last week in June. He was a little worried about going anywhere that close to the delivery date but everything was ready for the baby. The room and furniture were finished.

Some of Julie's friends at school had given her a baby shower before school ended and her mother and sister had a shower in Chicago for her and sent her all the presents. The baby had more than it would ever need or use, so Julie could leave for a week and not worry about things that needed to be done. Besides, he would be there to keep an eye on her and make sure she didn't overdo it.

Ben had booked a room for them at a resort in San Antonio. They were both excited as they packed the car and started their trip. Ben made sure he stopped every few hours so Julie could take a break. She had kept her weight down and didn't seem to be too uncomfortable during their drive. He had packed his medical bag with needed supplies just in case there should be a problem. They didn't arrive at the resort until that evening and by the time they had unloaded the car, Julie was so tired, they decided to order room service and then go to bed.

The next day they slept late and then went down to the restaurant for a late brunch. They went for a walk along the riverwalk and browsed in the shops. They stopped for an ice cream and then went back to the resort to spend the afternoon at the pool. Julie was embarrassed to even put on a swimsuit, so she just sat out in her shorts and sleeveless top. It was nice to just relax and read. Ben swam for a while and then took a nap in the sun. That evening they dressed up and went to a very nice Mexican restaurant along the river. They ate and danced and just enjoyed being together and talking.

Ben really treasured his time with Julie. He hoped that they would still have time to spend just with each other after the baby came. He knew it would be different, but he wanted them to at least go out alone once a week. He wasn't sure how Julie felt about that, however. He was afraid she would want to spend all her time with the baby. As he held her in his arms that night, he was a little melancholy thinking that soon their lives would change and never be the same.

The next day they decided to just relax around the pool and then do a little sightseeing that afternoon. After lunch Julie seemed a little tired so they decided to go to a movie and then out to dinner and to save the sight seeing for the next day. They had both soaked up a little too much sun, so a few hours in a cool moive theater felt good. It took them a while to decide on a place to eat because nothing sounded appetizing to Julie. They finally decided to go to a T.G.I. Friday's next to their hotel.

Julie slept late the next morning. Ben showered and went down for breakfast, just letting her sleep. He ordered her a sweet roll and some fruit to take back to the room but she wasn't hungry. She didn't seem to feel too well that entire day. They had planned to do some sight seeing but after he saw her slow down and grimace in pain several times, he told her they were going back to the hotel. He thought she might be starting labor but she said she didn't think so, that she was just tired. She napped most of the afternoon and he watched TV and read some. He wanted to go out by the pool but he was worried about her. After she woke up she seemed fine and they went to a wonderful Mexican restaurant that they had spotted that morning, for dinner.

After dinner, they decided to go to another movie. There were two that they had a hard time deciding between the day before. Julie could not seem to sit still during the movie. Ben could tell that she was very uncomfortable. She told him her back just hurt. By the time they got back to their room, she seemed so uncomfortable, he told her he wanted to examine her. He went to the car to get his bag and stopped by the drink machine to get some juice for her and by the time he got back he could tell without examining her that she was in labor.

He was so calm when he delivered other people's babies, but when he saw Julie on that bed, in labor, he became so nervous, he could hardly think what to do next. She told him that she had walked into the bathroom when he left the room and her water had broken. He examined her and she was already dilated 6 centimeters. He told her that he wasn't sure he had time to get her to the hospital that he might have to deliver the baby himself. He called the front desk and explained the situation. He asked them to bring up some clean towels and linens and several large bowls. He heated some water in the coffee pot in their room. He looked up the number to the nearest hospital and called the emergency room, explaining the situation and asking them to send an ambulance.

By the time he had done that, Julie was really in pain. He had seen this so many times but this was different. This was his Julie. He coached her in her breathing and rubbed her back. He wished he had a fetal monitor for the baby, to make sure everything was okay. He could tell that the baby was going to come before the ambulance got there, so he prepared her for delivery. She seemed calmer than he did. Someone had brought up the towels, sheets and two bowls and the water in the coffee pot was heated. With the supplies he had brought with him in his bag, he really had all he needed to deliver his child.

The next time he examined her, he could see the crown of the baby's head. He told her it was time and that now she could push. She was a real trooper. She pushed for about two or three minutes and he was holding his very own little daughter in his arms. He was crying and Julie was crying. He quickly counted all the toes and fingers and examined her the best he could. She seemed as healthy as any baby he had ever delivered and of course she was more beautiful than any other newborn he had ever seen. He suctioned the mucous from her mouth and wrapped her in a towel and gave her to Julie to hold while he cut and tied the umbilical cord and delivered the after birth. About the time he finished stitching Julie and cleaning her up, the ambulance arrived and he helped get her and the baby in the back and they all went to the hospital.

When they got to the hospital, he explained that he was a doctor and everything that had happened. They called in a pediatrician to examine the baby and checked Julie into a room. He consulted with the OB doctor on call and they agreed that she should stay in the hospital a few nights and if she and the baby were okay, they could both be checked out in a few days.

He checked with the Pediatrician, who told him that his little girl was as healthy as could be. They just had to do some blood work and then they would bring her to Julie's room. He then went back to be with Julie.

She was just beaming when he entered the room. He was so tired and could imagine how tired she was, but he was so wired and excited that he hardly felt the fatigue. The wonder and awe of bringing his own little girl into the world was just more than he could express. He went over and held Julie as she cried from exhaustion and happiness. He told her he was sorry that he had taken her away from home so close to delivery and she hushed him and said that she wouldn't have wanted it any other way. She was so glad that the first face their little girl saw when she entered the world was her father's.

They heard the door open and the nurse brought in the baby. She was all cleaned up and had such a pretty pink color. She had dark hair like Julie's and a lot of it. They had stuck a little pink bow in her hair. In Ben's eyes she was just perfect. For someone who wasn't sure he even wanted to be a father, his heart was completely taken with her.

They had decided that if it was a girl, they would name her Megan Elizabeth. Ben was so glad they had a little girl. He wanted a son eventually, but he was so glad that their first was a girl. They unwrapped her and looked at her whole, perfect, little body. Julie kept saying, "She's so tiny, our little Megan."

She was asleep when the nurse first brought her in, but it wasn't long before she opened her eyes and started crying. The nurse came in and helped Julie with her first attempt at nursing. Megan nursed with ease and then fell immediately back asleep. By that time, Julie seemed completely worn out. Ben left her and the baby sleeping and decided to go back to the hotel to shower and change and try to get some sleep himself. He also had phone calls to make to Julie's parents and his parents.

When he got back to the hotel room, it was completely cleaned up from the delivery the night before. He was eager to call Julie's parents but not so eager to call his. He knew his father and mother would get on his case for taking Julie on a trip so close to her deliver date. He decided to shower and then call Julie's parents first. He couldn't remember that a shower had ever felt so good. He hadn't realized how tired he was.

The Bennetts were surprised and a little worried, when he told them they were in San Antonio. He assured them mother and baby were fine and that they would probably be heading home, as soon as Julie and the baby were released from the hospital. They told him that they would make arrangements to fly to Houston by the end of the week, giving them a few days to get back home and settled before visiting. They were so excited as Ben described little Megan to them. They told him they would make their flight arrangements and he told them he would call them as soon as they were home to find out their schedule.

Ben then placed a call to his father and mother. They were not at home, as usual, so he left them a message on their answering machine. He never knew where they were or when they would be home, so he had no idea when they might know that they were grandparents. He wasn't expecting much from them except criticism of him anyway. He was actually glad they were not home to receive the message.

He was so exhausted, that after calling both sets of parents, he called the front desk to get a wake up call in four hours and was asleep as soon as his head hit the pillow. However, he only slept soundly for about two hours before having the nightmare that he hadn't had in years. He dreamed again of that first little girl that he helped abort and how she was crying and holding out her arms to him for help. There were scars over her face and hands from the saline solution and she seemed in such pain and agony. Then it wasn't her it was Megan that he saw in the dream crying for him to help her. He sat up in bed with his heart pounding and perspiration streaming down his face. He couldn't understand why he would have that dream again. He had been performing abortions for years and hadn't dreamt it. Why now? He was too troubled to go back to sleep and too worried about Megan. He got dressed and hurried back to the hospital.

He couldn't explain his feelings but he was so anxious that something might have happened to Megan. He drove to the hospital as fast as he could and ran up to Julie's room. He entered the room so quickly and with such a frightened look on his face, that it startled Julie who was nursing Megan. "What in the world's wrong," asked Julie? Ben didn't want to tell Julie about the dream, so he just told her that he woke up from a few hours sleep and was worried about her and the baby.

Julie had no idea how the dream had frightened him and she thought it was touching that he was so concerned for them. She assured him that other than trying to keep their little girl full, they were doing just great. He asked her if she had been able to rest any and she told him not much because there seemed to be someone coming in her room to check this or that all the time. Megan was asleep again and had stopped nursing so Julie asked Ben if he wanted to hold her. He hadn't really held her except for when he delivered her and in the ambulance for a few minutes.

He picked her up very gently in his arms and touched her soft little cheek. Already she was so precious to him. He hugged her gently to him, rocking her back and forth. The dream flashed back to his mind and he silently promised Megan that he would protect her and not ever let anyone hurt her. A lone tear ran down his cheek.

He was so lost in his thoughts and this overpowering love for his little girl that he didn't see how touched Julie was as she watched them. He looked up and saw her wiping tears from her eyes. He quickly went over to her to see if she was okay. "Are you feeling okay?" he asked with concern. She assured him that other than being tired she felt fine. She told him that she loved him more at that moment, as she watched him with Megan, than at any other time in their lives together. That's what caused the tears. She moved over on the bed and Ben sat beside her as he held Megan and watched her sleep. Ben told Julie that he never realized he would feel this way about a child. He told her that he had delivered so many babies that he had lost some of the wonder of birth. He wasn't consciously aware that it was not the many deliveries that he had performed that had caused him to loose the wonder of birth, but the many abortions.

Ben sat there on the bed with her for a few hours just holding Megan and talking. He told her that he had phoned her parents and how excited they were. They were going to try to get a flight that weekend to Houston. He hoped that Julie and Megan would be able to leave the hospital by the next day so that they would be able to get home and get adjusted a little before her parents came. The doctor was suppose to come in that afternoon and the pediatrician later that night so he would ask them. Then maybe they could make plans after talking with them. He told her that he didn't want to rush things and wanted to be sure the drive back to Houston wouldn't be too hard on them. All Julie wanted was to be at home and out of the hospital.

They didn't even have anything to dress Megan in when they left the hospital so Julie asked Ben if he would go to one of the shops they had looked in day before yesterday and buy her something to wear home. He also needed to buy some disposable diapers and diaper wipes. He gently put Megan in her bed and kissed Julie goodbye, promising to try and return before the doctor did his rounds.

Ben was glad to be out doing something. He thought maybe being more active would help get that dream out of his mind. He had a great time shopping. He bought a little pink dress and booties for Megan. He also bought a soft pink and white blanket. He got the diapers and wipes. That took him a while. He didn't realize there were so many name brands and sizes. Then he decided to buy Julie a new outfit to wear home from the hospital, since all she had with her were maternity clothes. It took him a while on hers, because he wasn't sure what size to get. He finally decided on a matching knit shirt and shorts outfit that looked like it was suppose to fit loosely.

He was later getting back to the hospital than he had hoped. By the time he got to Julie's room the OB doctor had already been in. Julie told him that she would be ready to be dismissed by noon tomorrow. The doctor had checked her and everything seemed fine. If the pediatrician okayed Megan's release they could be on their way home by 1:00 or 2:00. Ben showed Julie what he had bought for her and the baby.

She hadn't even thought about what she would wear home and was appreciative that he had thought of getting her a new outfit. She just hoped she would fit into it. To Ben she didn't even look like she had ever been pregnant. He thought she was the most beautiful woman he had ever seen. He was about to take her in his arms and tell her that when the Pediatrician came into the room.

He examined Megan and talked to them a few minutes. He told them that she could go home the next day also. She was in perfect health. Ben visited until after dinner that night and then promised Julie he would pack up the car and be there before noon to pick her and Megan up. They were both so excited to be going home.

Chapter 16

They didn't arrive home until late the next night. Ben still had several days vacation which was good because they were all very tired. The long ride home had been hard for Julie. Megan didn't sleep good that first night home, probably because she was in a different environment. He didn't have to get up when she woke because Julie was nursing her but he woke up each time she cried, so he got up several times and brought her to Julie to nurse.

Julie's mother and father were coming in two days. He was glad they had not been able to book a flight until then because he would enjoy just having the next two days to enjoy being alone with his little family. However, it would be nice to have Julie's mother there to help. He would have to be back at work then and he felt much better leaving Julie knowing that her parents were there.

He just couldn't get enough of looking at Megan. She was so little and perfect. She looked so much like Julie with her dark hair and creamy skin. They both tried to nap when Megan was sleeping so getting up during the night those first two days back didn't bother them too much.

Ben picked Julie's parents up at the airport Saturday morning. They could hardly wait to see Julie and the baby. It was the fastest he'd ever gotten out of the airport when picking them up. They agreed with him that Megan was the most beautiful little girl in the whole world. Julie just beamed as they all oohed and ahhed over her. They just relaxed and visited most of the afternoon.

Ben had planned to call and order some dinner from the Italian place down the street but Mrs. Bennett insisted that she cook dinner. "After all," she said, "I came to help." She fixed a wonderful dinner of fried chicken, mashed potatoes, green beans and homemade biscuits. Megan was sleeping peacefully and they had just sat down to eat when the doorbell rang.

Ben couldn't believe his eyes; his parents were standing at the door! He stood there a minute without saying anything. Then he found his voice and asked them in. Julie and her parents seemed very excited to see them. He didn't say much, as they explained that they had business in California on Monday and had decided to detour and stop by Houston to see the baby for the weekend.

He wanted to tell them they could have at least called, but he was too mad to say anything. Julie spoke up and offered to set them a place for dinner, but they said they had already eaten at the airport and that all they wanted to do was see their new little granddaughter. Dinner was delayed while Ben and Julie took them into the bedroom to see Megan.

His mother wouldn't leave well enough alone and just look at her, she had to pick her up and awaken her. She held her for a few minutes until she started crying and then she quickly handed her to Julie. Julie changed and fed her before they finally got to sit down and eat. What had started out as a pleasant quiet meal with just Julie's parents, ended up, in Ben's opinion, to be a fiasco.

When they went to bed that night, Julie asked him why he had seemed so irritated all evening. He wasn't even sure he knew, but tried to explain to her that he resented his parents interrupting their time with her parents and that he thought it extremely rude that they didn't even call first. Julie tried to calm him some and told him that they should be glad his parents cared enough to want to see Megan. She didn't mind them being there for the weekend and she was sure her parents didn't mind. Besides her parents would be there the whole week and his parents were only there for two days.

Sometimes it irritated Ben that Julie was so loving and understanding about everything. If he wanted to be mad at his parents, he would be mad. Besides they never seemed to like little babies before now. Why were they so interested, all of a sudden, in being the devoted grandparents? He lay awake in bed for a long time just thinking of all the reasons he resented their visit. He finally fell asleep only to be awakened by Megan an hour later. That's pretty much how the whole night went.

He did manage to wake up the next morning in a little better humor. Julie's mom was already up cooking breakfast when he got up. Julie was sitting in the kitchen with her mom, feeding Megan. He asked where Mr. Bennett was and Julie said he had walked down the street to the little quick shop to get a paper.

Ben knew without asking that his parents were still sleeping. They were not early risers on the weekend. In fact, his mother was never an early riser. He was hoping they would sleep through breakfast, but just as the food was put on the table they came out to join them. Breakfast was pleasant enough but Ben wondered what they were going to do the rest of the day. He was surprised at how much attention his mother gave Megan throughout the day. His father spent most of the day on the phone.

That afternoon, they wanted him to show them his practice. He didn't particularly want to but it would get them out of the house for a while and give Julie a break. His father asked him a million questions on the way to his office, none of which he thought was any of his business. His mother tried to change the subject asking him about Julie and the delivery. He told them about getting to deliver Megan in the hotel room. His mother found that disgusting and his father immediately told him how stupid it was to take a trip that close to her delivery. They arrived at his office, just as he was ready to explode. At least his parents had positive things to say about the practice. He showed them around as quickly as he could and told them that he was anxious to get back and spend some time with Julie as he had to be back at work the next day.

They stopped and picked up some Chinese food on the way home. Dinner was actually uneventful. Ben didn't talk much, but Julie and the Bennetts kept things lively. Megan woke up during dinner so Julie didn't get to finish her meal. They watched some T.V. that night and all decided to go to bed early. His parents had a 9:00 flight and he had to be in the office by 7:30.

As they got ready for bed, Julie commented on what a nice visit it had been with his parents. He didn't want to burst her bubble, but they were only nice as long as they were around she and her parents. He didn't tell her about the conversation they'd had on the way to his office. However, they did seem to be smitten with Megan. He didn't under-stand it, given their lack of attention to him growing up, and he certainly didn't expect it to last. He just agreed with Julie, so she wouldn't know how he really felt.

He told her how he hated to go back to work the next day. He wished he had a few more days to stay at home with her and Megan. They went to sleep holding each other close, in a much more loving mood than the night before.

Ben was up early but Mrs. Bennett had beat him up and had breakfast ready for him. His parents joined them before leaving for the airport. Just before they were ready to leave, Julie brought Megan out, after feeding her, to tell everyone goodbye. Ben hugged them close and promised to get home from work as soon as possible. His mother held Megan and actually seemed sad to leave. His father was in his usual hurry. He was later leaving than he had wanted, so he told his parents a hurried goodbye and rushed out the door.

His patient load that day was unbelievable. He had wanted to get home by 6:00 but didn't end up leaving the office until 7:00. When he got home, everyone had waited on him for dinner and Julie was feeding Megan. He was so glad to be home. He had really missed Julie and Megan. They had a nice quiet evening. He enjoyed having Julie's parents there. They were so unintrusive, and unlike his parents, they were so helpful. Julie gave Megan to him to hold while she helped her mother get dinner on the table. He couldn't believe how much she already seemed a part of their lives. Everytime he looked at her, he was just overwhelmed with love. Sometimes the dream that he had the day after Megan was born came back to mind and he would draw her closer to him, vowing to protect her.

The rest of the week went much the same. His schedule slowed down a little toward the end of the week. He did have more of a problem at the abortion clinic than he'd had in a long time. He had to really work at convincing himself that this was only tissue and not a baby yet. He'd even had that nightmare once, the night after he worked at the clinic. He finally talked himself into believing that these babies would not have been wanted even if they had been born. It was totally different than Megan whom they both had planned for and wanted.

He and Julie both hated to see her parents go that Saturday. There were so many hugs and kisses that he was afraid they were going to miss their plane. As usual, Julie cried all the way home from the airport. He had learned to just let her cry and hold and comfort her as much as he could.

Chapter 17

As the weeks went by, their lives seemed to get back into a routine. However, he could tell Julie was not looking forward to teaching that fall. They talked about it a lot over the summer months and they decided that if she increased her private students, they could afford for her not to teach until Megan was older. This made Ben glad he had agreed to work at the abortion clinic. There was no way they could have afforded the house payment and their other payments this early in his career, on his salary, had he not been working at the clinic.

He had been having difficulty performing the abortions since Megan was born, but this was a way for him to justify it to himself. Because he was working at the clinic, Julie was able to stay home with Megan. Besides, they had increased the amount they charged at the abortion clinic that year and he was beginning to bring home more income from that than his practice, plus it took up less of his time. Once again, he compartmentalized his thoughts and justified his actions.

As that first year after Megan's birth passed, he tried to spend more time during the evenings and weekends at home. He wanted to share in as much of her life as possible. He was never unwilling to change diapers, feed her or bathe her. His favorite part was rocking her for a while each night. He would talk to her and even though she couldn't talk, she would look up at him and coo and smile. She had captured his heart from the moment she was born but as each day passed and she was able to respond to him better, he adored her more and more.

As he spent time with Megan, he would often wonder how his parents could have remained so distant from him while he was growing up. It was such an amazing thing to be a parent. Each stage of development that first year was new and exciting. He was always eager to come home and hear about what feats she had accomplished that day. From her first smile, to learning to turn over and crawl, to her first tooth were all reasons for celebration.

As Megan approached her first birthday, Ben was amazed at how much she favored Julie. She was so beautiful with a head full of soft, black curls and big, blue eyes with long black eyelashes. She had the softest and most beautiful colored complexion and big dimples when she smiled. They would be in a store or out eating and people would stop and comment on what a beautiful baby she was. Her personality was like Julie's also. She was cheerful and happy most of the time, unless she was hungry or wet. She loved everyone and never seemed to meet a stranger. He got a big kick out of how people just seemed to be drawn to her. She loved Julie and Julie was a wonderful mother, but she adored him. She had just started walking and whenever he walked in the door , she would toddle over to him with her arms outstretched saying, "Da Da."

Julie's parents planned to come for Megan's birthday. He wasn't sure if any of Julie's other family members were going to be able to come, except David. They had spent Christmas at Julie's parents and had seen her whole family then. It had been a fun and exciting Christmas. Everyone loved and doted on Megan. Tommy and Ashley had just found out that they were going to have a baby in August, so he doubted they would be traveling with her in her eighth month. Stephanie had received an engagement ring from Peter that Christmas and they were going to get married the following February. They would get to see everyone when they went to Chicago for the wedding. Carl might come with his parents, but he had just graduated that Spring and had started a new job. So, as far as they knew, only Mr and Mrs. Bennett and David were coming.

A few days before Megan's birthday, his parents called and said they would like to come. Julie had answered the phone and told them that they would love to have them. She made Ben promise that he would not act like he had the last time they visited and that he would just relax and try and enjoy everyone. He promised he would try because he did want it to be a special first birthday for Megan.

Both his parents and Julie's family arrived the day before Megan's birthday. It took a while to get everyone settled and they all went out for dinner that evening. His parents seemed in a pleasant, non-critical mood, so they really did have a nice dinner. Megan, of course, captured everyone's attention, including his parents. They thought she was the most beautiful child on the face of the earth, but Megan's favorite person was David. From the moment she laid eyes on him, she followed him around everywhere. He loved her too but he wasn't quite sure how to react to her.

The next day everyone awakened around 8:00. Julie had planned to cook-out for lunch and then have a cake and ice cream for Megan's birthday. She had an overabundance of presents. Tommy and Ashley had sent her something, Carl had mailed a present, Stephanie sent one by her parents and even David had bought her something himself. Mr. and Mrs. Bennett gave her a new outfit and a toy, while Julie's brothers and sister all sent clothes, except for David who gave her a big, stuffed teddy bear.

His parents had gone completely overboard. They gave her several very expensive little outfits and a big plastic play gym set for outside. At first, Ben was embarrassed that they had bought such elaborate presents, but no one else seemed to mind and he knew Megan would love the outdoor set. Especially as she got a little older. They had a fun cook-out and Megan loved her birthday cake. They put it on her highchair and just let her dig into it. Everyone sang happy birthday as she laughed and clapped. Everyone took pictures and he took a video of the whole thing.

When it came time to open the presents, she was more interested in the paper and boxes than the presents. By the time she finished she needed a nap and so did the rest of them. In fact, Julie put Megan to bed and after cleaning up, the rest of them decided to take a nap, everyone but David. He stayed up and watched a baseball game on TV.

Megan only slept an hour, probably from all the sugar she'd had that day. Ben, Mr. Bennett and David spent part of the afternoon putting together the outdoor playground. Ben expected his father to help, since it was their present to Megan, but he spent his time making business phone calls. They did bring Megan outside when it was finally put together and played with her on it for a while. They had a late dinner and then all watched a movie they had rented. Much to Ben's surprise, it had been a pleasant day. His parents had been relatively easy to get along with. Maybe Julie was partially right and he just needed to change his attitude in order to make things better. They did seem to love Megan and she loved them.

They had to leave the next day, but Julie's family weren't leaving until the following weekend. Ben even offered to drive them to the airport. In fact, Julie suggested the two of them drive them and leave Megan with her parents. They had a nice leisurely breakfast the next morning and then Mr. and Mrs. Strickland packed to go. Megan gave them each a hug goodbye and blew them a kiss as they left. Ben thought he saw a tear in his mother's eye as they got in the car. He had to admit that if anyone could touch someone's heart, it was Megan. The drive to the airport was pleasant. They helped get the luggage out of the car and waited in the airport with them until they boarded their plane. It was always easier to get along with them when Julie was around, so Ben was glad she had offered to come with him.

Julie's parents had suggested that he and Julie take the afternoon to do something fun together and they would watch Megan, since they hardly had any time with just the two of them. Before Megan was born, Ben had worried that Julie wouldn't ever want to just spend time with him anymore. However, it was usually him that didn't want to leave Megan with a babysitter, not Julie. Julie thought the afternoon out together was a great idea, so they had lunch at one of their favorite Italian restaurants and then they shopped a little and went to an afternoon movie. It really was great just to be out with Julie for a while. It seemed like they hardly had any time to just talk and enjoy each other any more. Of course, most of their conversation centered around Megan. Julie did thank him for being so pleasant around his parents. He admitted that he had kind of enjoyed their visit this time. Julie hoped that maybe this was the beginning of a better relationship between he and his parents. Maybe Megan would be that bridge that drew them together.

The afternoon seemed to fly by. They both enjoyed it so much. They picked up a few groceries on the way home and had planned to grill out some chicken but when they got back to their house, Mrs. Bennett already had dinner prepared. Julie gave her mother a big hug. They both thanked them profusely for watching Megan and giving them some time alone. Julie helped her mother get dinner on the table, while Ben put away the groceries. They had a pleasant dinner with David and Megan both keeping them well entertained.

Ben had to go to work the next morning but the whole week with Julie's parents and David was very enjoyable. He knew Julie loved having them around. She grew up in such a large household that the more people around, the better she liked it. Megan loved it even more. By the end of the week she had grown very attached to them. When they got on their plane the next Saturday, Megan cried and they cried. Julie didn't cry as much this time because she was trying to get Megan to calm down. However, she was sad because she knew they wouldn't see them this next Christmas because they were going to wait and go home for Stephanie's wedding in February. They had both agreed it would be nice to spend this Christmas in their own home, but it seemed like such a long time until February.

Chapter 18

B en spent the rest of that year working a lot longer hours than he wanted. However, he knew that it would be even worse if he wasn't making the money he did at the abortion clinic. He continued to have his nightmare about that first abortion every now and then, but it grew less and less frequent.

Julie continued teaching her private piano lessons. At this point he was making enough that they were able to put the money she made and part of his income from the clinic into savings. He wanted to eventually build a house, but Julie never seemed to want to talk about leaving where they were. He wanted to move into a little more prestigious neighborhood. He had also started buying savings bonds for Megan's education. Ben was beginning to feel pretty good about their financial situation.

Julie had been talking about wanting to have another baby ever since Megan's birthday. He thought they should wait to even consider it until Megan was at least two or three years old. He kept trying to explain that he just wanted to enjoy Julie and Megan for a while. He didn't tell Julie this but he also wanted to have a few more years to save. However, Julie said that if they started trying now, maybe they would have another child about the time Megan turned two. She didn't want there to be too much difference in their ages. He was perfectly happy with just Julie and Megan but he didn't want Megan to grow up as an only child the way he had, so he never really settled it with Julie. He just kept telling her that maybe they should try soon but not right then. However, by that Christmas Julie had a surprise announcement for him.

Ben was on call Christmas Eve. He did get to have dinner at home, before being paged by the hospital. They had bought Megan several toys that had to be put together so he hoped he wouldn't be at the hospital all night. He ended up getting home around 11:00. Julie had a fire in the fireplace and some hot cider and cookies waiting for him. They sat in front of the fire just enjoying each other and their snack for a while, then Ben made himself get up and put Megan's toys together before he fell asleep sitting there on the couch with Julie.

While he assembled the little riding toy and a playhouse, Julie stuffed their stockings. That was always her favorite part of getting Christmas ready. She bought little things all throughout the year, whenever she saw something he might like or she thought would be good for Megan. They always did their stockings first on Christmas morning. He did Julie's after he finished the toys. By 12:30, they were ready to go to bed. They were both exhausted and knew Megan would be up bright and early.

She woke up at 6:00. She was just beginning to understand about Christmas and knew that there would be presents downstairs for her. She was so excited about everything she saw. She wasn't sure which thing to play with first. They had so much fun watching her, they almost forgot their presents to each other. Julie gave Ben an old antique clock for his office. He loved old clocks and had quite a collection of them. It was beautiful, unlike any he had ever seen. She also bought him a new pair of pants, a shirt, a sweater and a new Tom Clancey book he had been wanting to read. He gave her a new charm for her bracelet and a new gown and robe. He also bought her a new pair of jeans, two sweaters and a very stylish pants suit.

They had fun opening their stockings. He had her favorite perfume in hers slong with a pocket calendar, some new earrings and some of her favorite candies. She had stuffed his with candy and fruit, a new pen set, a new tie and a blue bubble gum cigar. He couldn't figure that one out for a while and then it hit him. He turned to see her with a big smile on her face. "You're not, are you," he asked? She ran over and threw her arms around him and assured him that she was going to have their second child.

Ben wasn't as excited as he thought he would be. He tried to act that way for Julie, but as he looked at little Megan playing and thought how perfect their lives seemed, he wasn't sure he wanted another child right then. However, he mustered up a big hug and smile for Julie and convinced her that he was thrilled.

As much as he didn't want Megan to be an only child, as he had been, he just couldn't seem to feel excitement about Julie's announcement. In fact, it bothered him the rest of that day. Why couldn't they just leave well enough alone for right now. Their lives seemed to be so perfect. He seemed to have this consistent fear that something was going to come along to destroy all that he held dear. His feelings were not logical and they didn't even make sense to him. He knew he would love any child that belonged to he and Julie. However, he couldn't imagine loving another baby as much as he loved Megan.

Chapter 19

The next few months were not easy ones. Unlike her first pregnancy, Julie was sick most of the time. She seemed worn out and pale all of the time. He would come home from work and find her trying to prepare dinner in between running to the bathroom to be sick. He tried to spend as much time as he could at home helping her but she just didn't seem to have any energy.

He decided to hire a woman to come in and help a few days a week. Julie was not pleased with this at first but he finally convinced her that if she had help around the house, she would have more energy to spend time with Megan. She finally agreed and seemed to feel a little better for the next several weeks. However he was still concerned about her.

The doctor told them everything seemed okay but Ben was worried about her. This pregnancy seemed to being so different than the last one. He had been a doctor long enough to know that each pregnancy was different but something just didn't seem right about this one.

Ben wasn't sure they should try to travel to Stephanie's wedding, but he knew Julie would never agree to not go. Besides, she was suppose to be the Matron of Honor and Megan was going to be the flower girl. They were going to get there a few days before the wedding so they could make sure their dresses fit. Julie hadn't gained much weight because she was sick most of the time. She hoped she could make it through the wedding without being sick. She was so excited about going and seeing her whole family. They hadn't even seen Tom and Ashley's little baby, Matthew. He was excited also, but worried about Julie.

Their flight seemed to go okay and Julie actually made it without being sick. Her parents were at the airport to pick them up. There were many hugs and kisses as usual. Megan definitely remembered her Grandma and Grandpa. She was so excited to see them. When they got to the Bennett's house, nothing had changed except that there seemed to be more people in it than ever. As the family increased in number the house seemed to decrease in size.

Ben and Julie were staying at a nearby hotel along with Tom, Ashley and Matthew. However, the Bennetts planned a big buffet dinner that night with the whole family. It was great seeing everyone again. Little Matthew seemed so small compared to Megan. However, he was six months old and beginning to crawl. Megan was intrigued with him. She would talk to him and try and help him move to get what he wanted. Ben was very proud of how she shared with him. They only stayed a while after dinner because he could tell Julie was tired and she had already been sick several times since dinner. They went back to their hotel and she fell into bed. He told her to just rest and he would get Megan to bed. By the time Megan was asleep Julie was also fast asleep.

The next few days were very hectic. Julie and Megan were fitted for their dresses the next morning. Megan was so excited as she tried on her beautiful dress. She was not quite two years old but already loved to dress up. After the dress fittings, she went shopping with Stephanie and her mother. They all had dinner together again at the Bennett's house that night. The next night was the rehearsal dinner and then the wedding was at 2:00 Saturday afternoon.

It was a beautiful wedding. Megan looked so cute walking slowly down the aisle throwing flower petals. She looked over at Ben once and he thought she was going to come over to him but she just smiled and waved. He waved back and had to hold back the tears. She was so precious to him. Sometimes he had this tremendous wave of protectiveness towards Megan wash over him. He just wanted to pick her up and hug her to him and not let anything in life ever hurt her.

He looked up at Julie, already in place at the front of the church, and she was smiling at Megan, urging her with her eyes to continue down the aisle. They were so much alike and he loved them both with his whole being. The reception was a block away at the same place he and Julie had had their reception. It brought back memories. He'd never been happier at any time in his life than he was right now. His life seemed so complete. Sometimes he forgot they were going to add another child to their family. He was happy just the way they were.

Julie almost didn't make it through the reception. She was sick several times, but tried not to draw attention to herself. She didn't want to take anything away from Stephanie's day. Therefore, Ben didn't know how bad she had been feeling until they got back to their hotel late that evening.

He put Megan to bed and then went into the bathroom to find Julie pale as a ghost and very sick to her stomach. He told her he was going to the drugstore to get her some medicine for her nausea and made her promise to sleep late the next morning. She was up off and on all night. Ben was really beginning to worry about her. She hadn't been nearly this sick with Megan. When he woke up the next morning she was finally sleeping, so he got Megan dressed and took her to a McDonald's nearby for breakfast. She wanted to know why they left Mommy behind so he explained to her that Mommy wasn't feeling good so they were going to let her rest. After they ate, he let her play on the playground for a while, to give Julie a few extra hours sleep. She seemed a little better when they returned to the hotel. She had a little more color in her face.

They were suppose to fly home that afternoon, so they packed up before Mr. Bennett came by to get them, around 11:00. They were going to have lunch with Julie's family and then her mom and dad were taking them to the airport. Ben noticed that Julie hardly ate anything for lunch. This was her third month of pregnancy and he knew the nausea was usually the worst during the first trimester. Hopefully, by next month, she would be feeling much better.

They had a nice final lunch with her family. Stephanie and Peter had left for their honeymoon the night before but the rest of the family was still there. Ben really enjoyed each member of Julie's family and could understand why she always hated to leave. Megan was having so much fun, that they had to almost drag her to the car to go to the airport. She was excited about flying on the plane again, however. She had been very good on the way to Chicago. The stewardess brought her some wings to wear and some crayons and a coloring book.

The flight back was not quite so easy. Megan was unusually whiny because she wanted Grandpa and Grandma to come with them and Julie had to keep running to the bathroom because she was sick again. By the time they landed, they were all exhausted. All they'd had to eat on the plane was peanuts and soda and Julie hadn't eaten any of that. They were going to stop and get a bite to eat on the way home, but Julie told Ben she just didn't think she could sit through a meal in a restaurant. They went home and she went straight to bed.

Ben knew she must really be feeling bad not to even worry about what he and Megan were going to eat for dinner. Every ounce of energy seemed drained from her. He made her promise, before she went to bed, that she would call her doctor the next day and have him check her. In fact, he intended to call and talk to him from his office the next morning.

He unloaded the car and then fixed he and Megan some soup and a sandwich. She was tired from all the travel too so he read her a bedtime story and put her to bed shortly after dinner. Ben cleaned up the kitchen and had just sat down to watch the news for a while before going to bed, when he heard Julie scream for him from the bathroom. He ran to the bathroom with his heart in his throat.

When he got there Julie, was bent over double in pain. He helped her to the bed and elevated her feet, Frantically, he called several of their sitters before he was able to find someone to come and watch Megan at the last minute. Then he helped Julie to the car and drove her to the hospital. The whole way there she was sobbing and saying she hoped she didn't lose their baby.

Ben was more worried about her and just kept trying to calm her and comfort her. It seemed like an eternity before he got her there. He had called her doctor before leaving their house so he was there to meet them. Ben was there holding Julie's hand while he examined her. He told them that he was afraid Julie might have an ectopic pregnancy and wanted to send them for a sonogram. Julie had calmed down a little but Ben saw tears forming in her eyes again. The sonogram showed a ruptured fallopian tube so they got Julie ready for surgery immediately. Julie clung to him as they wheeled her to surgery. He was sad about loosing their child but mostly he was worried about Julie. He knew that when the tube ruptured it could be serious.

He called, while Julie was in surgery, to tell their sitter that he would be at the hospital most of the night. He wasn't sure whether to call Mr. And Mrs. Bennett now or after the surgery. He finally decided that they should know in case something went wrong.

When they answered the phone they thought Ben was just calling them to let them know they had arrived home safely. They were shocked when he told them Julie was in surgery. He explained the best he could what had happened and they were devastated. They asked how Julie was and he told them she had lost a lot of blood and was still in surgery. They wanted to get a flight and come the next day, but Ben asked them to wait and let him see how Julie was first.

After hanging up with the Bennetts, Ben was headed to surgery when he saw Julie's doctor. He told Ben that she had lost a lot of blood and was weak but would be okay. He assured Ben that they had only had to remove her left tube and that they would be able to have other children.

For some reason it hadn't hit Ben yet that they had even lost a child, he was so concerned about Julie. He went immediately to recovery. Julie was still sleeping so he just stood beside her and held her hand. She looked so pale but so beautiful. Tears came to his eyes and he squeezed her hand as he wondered what he would ever do without her. As a doctor, he should have picked up on this pregnancy not being right and should have insisted on her having an ultrasound. He had just been so busy before the wedding pulling some extra on calls for his associates so that they would do the same for him while he was gone that he just thought she was having typical morning sickness.

Julie began to wake up after about an hour. The first thing she asked about was the baby. Ben wasn't sure whether she was just groggy or she hadn't understood that there was no way to save the baby in an ectopic pregnancy. He explained to her that the fetus was lodged in the fallopian tube and the tube had ruptured. She'd had emergency surgery and that there was no way to save the baby.

As weak as Julie was she burst into tears. She was crying hysterically when he called the nurse to give her something to calm her. He held her as close as he could with all the IV's and tubes and tried to comfort her. He told her they would have other children and that she must just concentrate on getting well for he and Megan. As she fell asleep she asked about Megan and he assured her he had called the sitter and she was fine.

Ben left to call Mr and Mrs. Bennett while Julie slept. They must have been waiting by the phone because they picked it up on the first ring. Ben assured them that Julie had come through the surgery fine and that he felt she would be okay. He told them that she seemed very upset when she woke up in recovery and found out she had lost the baby. Mrs. Bennett had already called and made plane reservations for the next day and told Ben that she could stay as long as he and Julie needed her help. Ben thanked her and told her that he felt Julie really did need her now. It would probably be at least several weeks before Julie was up and able to handle Megan and the house on her own. He wished he could be home with her but he couldn't be away from his practice or the clinic any longer. He'd already been gone a week.

Ben went back to recovery to find Julie awake. She wasn't crying anymore but she looked so sad. She wouldn't even say anything to him as he stood by her side. She just held his hand tight as tears filled her eyes again. She turned her head away from him. The nurse came before he could say anything and told him that all her vital signs were stable, so they would be moving her to a private room.

He walked beside her as they moved her out of recovery and took her to the 7th floor. Shortly after they had her settled in her room, she closed her eyes and Ben could tell that she had drifted off to sleep again. He decided that he should go home and shower and let the babysitter go home. Besides, Megan would be waking up soon and he needed to be there to explain where Julie was and that she would be home soon. Maybe he could even get a few hours sleep before Megan woke up. He hadn't even thought about it in the last few hours but he was exhausted.

When Ben arrived home, the babysitter was asleep and he quietly went to his room and showered. He set his clock for 6:30 and even though he was still worried about Julie, fell into an exhausted sleep. It seemed like his head had just touched the pillow when the alarm went off. He pulled himself from the bed and went to the kitchen to start a pot of coffee, before checking on Megan. Katherine, their sitter, was up by the time he had finished starting the coffee. She asked him how Julie was and told him she would go ahead and leave if that was okay because she would then have time to get home and get ready for school on time. Ben thanked her and paid her for the evening. She asked him if he would need her to watch Megan after school but he told her that Julie's mother would be arriving later that morning.

By the time Katherine left, Ben heard Megan awake in her room. He poured himself a cup of coffee and went upstairs to check on her. She was all sleepy eyed and sweet in the mornings. She held out her arms to him and as he picked her up and carried her downstairs, she gave him a big hug and kiss. She could always melt Ben's heart in a moment.

Ben could tell she was puzzled when they got downstairs because Julie was not in the kitchen as she normally was. "Where's Mommy?" Megan asked. Ben had poured them both a bowl of cereal and some juice and he reached over and took her hand as he explained that Mommy had not felt well the night before and he had taken her to the hospital to get all fixed up. "When will Mommy come home?" Megan asked with tears beginning to form in her big blue eyes. Ben explained to her that Mommy would have to rest in the hospital for a few days but that she would be home soon and that Grandma Bennett would come later that day to take care of her until Mommy was home again. That seemed to brighten Megan up considerably. She was really excited when Ben told her that they needed to hurry and eat breakfast and then she could go with him to his office for a little while until they went to the airport to pick up Grandma Bennett. Megan loved airplanes and talked about nothing else the rest of breakfast.

Ben still had one day of vacation but wanted to stop by his office to check his patient load for the next day, before going to the airport to pick up Mrs. Bennett. He hated to take Megan with him but didn't have time to try and find another sitter on such short notice. She was very good, however. She had only been to Ben's office a few times with Julie but he gave her a piece of paper and some colored pens and sat her on a chair in his office and she entertained herself, while he checked his schedule and called the hospital to check and see how Julie was. He talked to the nurse, who told him that she had rested pretty well through the night but that she had refused breakfast that morning. She told him that Julie had been asking for him.

He then rang Julie's room. He didn't think she was going to answer at first, but when she did, it didn't even sound like her. She was so quiet and subdued. He explained to her that he would be there as soon as he picked up her mother at the airport. She just said okay and didn't even ask any questions about how Megan was or about her mother coming.

Megan kept up a constant chatter on the way to the airport, but Ben wasn't really listening. His mind was on Julie. She had seemed so down. He knew she must be in a lot of pain and maybe she was still groggy from the surgery but there seemed to be more than that in her voice when he talked to her. Actually, there didn't seem to be any feeling at all in her voice. That's what worried him.

It didn't even occur to Ben that she was grieving over the loss of their child until, on the way back from the airport when Mrs. Bennett said that Julie must be so upset over loosing the baby. Ben had been doing abortions for so long now that he didn't really think of what had happened to Julie last night as losing their child. He didn't think of it as a child yet. It was just misplaced tissue to him and had caused Julie to be very ill. Even after Mrs. Bennett had asked about Julie's grief, he didn't feel anything about the baby that they had lost. He couldn't get himself to see it as a child. Not until the pregnancy was further along. He was just thankful that Julie was going to be okay.

Ben stopped by the hospital on the way home, so Mrs. Bennett could visit Julie a little while before he took she and Megan back to their house. He stayed down in the cafeteria with Megan and bought her an ice cream to give Mrs. Bennett some time with her daughter. He hoped her being there would help to cheer Julie up.

It was almost an hour before Mrs. Bennett met them back in the cafeteria. He could tell she had been crying but she tried to seem cheerful around Megan. However, when they were back home and Megan was playing up in her room, Mrs. Bennett pulled Ben aside before he left for the hospital and told him how concerned she was about Julie. She told him that she was sure Julie would be fine medically, but she was concerned about her emotionally.

Ben knew that the surgery had been major and that it would take some time for Julie to recover fully. He also knew that she had wanted another child, but this wasn't even a pregnancy that could have ever worked. He knew that her hormones were going through some major changes and he understood all the medical reasons why she might be a little depressed but he still could not understand what Mrs. Bennett termed as grief over their lost child.

He assured Mrs. Bennett that he would do all he could to help Julie cheer up. His idea of doing that was to be as cheerful as he could, while visiting her that afternoon. He came into the room with a smile on his face and had brought her some magazines that she liked and a beautiful new nightgown. She still looked so pale to him but he knew that was from the loss of blood. He tried to joke with her and tell her some of the cute things Megan had said to Mrs. Bennett that morning, but nothing he said or did brought a smile to her face. In fact, he hardly got any reaction at all. She answered whatever questions he asked but in a monotone voice and then was silent. The more cheerful he tried to be, the more tearful she became.

He stayed until her dinner was brought to her room and then she told him to go ahead and go home to be with Megan. He made her promise to eat something and told her that he would come by early tomorrow, before he went to the office and then again when he did rounds in the afternoon. He kissed her goodbye, really believing that as soon as Julie recovered physically she would be back to her normal self emotionally.

Chapter 20

However, that was not the case. Julie was in the hospital five days. She came home that Saturday and only brightened up a little when she saw Megan. Megan wanted to jump up in her lap and give her a big hug but Ben had to warn her that she had to be careful when hugging Mommy and not hurt where her surgery was. She did respond to Megan and they spent some time talking as Megan told her all she had done with Grandma Bennett that week. However, whenever Megan wasn't around, she went back into her hole and would barely respond to Ben. He could not figure out how to get Julie out of this depression.

It had been a few weeks since Julie came home from the hosptital and she seemed to go deeper and deeper into her depression. She didn't ever want to eat and was loosing more and more weight. She still tried to smile some around Megan, but with Ben she was very distant and quiet. Julie's mother was still with them and said she would stay as long as Ben and Julie needed her too. She was also very worried about Julie.

Ben finally decided to talk to Julie's mother after she had been home for a few weeks and still looked so pale and acted so withdrawn. Julie went to bed as soon as Megan was asleep each night. So, after she was in bed that evening, Ben sought out Mrs. Bennett in the kitchen. She was doing the dishes from dinner. He sat at the kitchen table and just carried on light conversation with her until she was done and then he asked her to sit at the table with him so he could discuss something with her.

Ben shared with her how puzzled and worried he was that Julie seemed to be recovering physically but not emotionally. "She barely responds to me anymore," Ben told her with a catch in his voice. Mrs. Bennett was worried also but she told Ben that Julie had really wanted this child and that it was very hard for a woman to know she was carrying a child and then lose it. She told him that Julie still loved him and needed him. In fact, she suggested that instead of trying to be so cheerful all the time, maybe he should sit and talk with Julie and let her share her grief with him.

Ben had been spending so much time trying to be cheerful around Julie that he really hadn't tried to talk to her about the way she felt. He knew she had wanted another child but they could still have children and he didn't see this as the loss of a child. If Julie had carried it full term and it had been born dead then he believed that he would have grieved too, but there was no way this fetus could be carried to full term.

He did need to get Julie to talk, however. He missed their closeness so much that he didn't care what he had to do to get her back to the way things were before her surgery. Maybe he had been looking at this whole thing too much from a medical point of view and missing what Julie was going through.

He gave Mrs. Bennett a hug and told her that he would make a point of talking to Julie the next day. In fact he told her that he would come home for lunch and maybe she could take Megan to the park for a while giving them some time to talk. She thought that was an excellent idea. Ben felt better already as he and Mrs. Bennett went into the den to watch TV for a while before going to bed.

Julie was just waking up as he went to work the next morning. He had gotten up and eaten breakfast with Megan and then came back in the bedroom to check on Julie before leaving. He gave her a kiss goodbye and she just turned her head away. This kind of response just broke Ben's heart. Julie had always been such a warm and loving person. In fact, she was the one who had taught Ben how to be loving and responsive and now she continued to shut him out.

He could hardly keep his mind on what went on at the clinic that morning. All he could think of was seeing Julie at lunch and trying to make her open up to him. He managed to get through the morning's abortions. In fact, he didn't even have to think about the procedure anymore. He had performed so many, since starting work at the clinic, that without him knowing it, he had become almost as cold about it as Dr. Williams had been that first day Ben had observed at the clinic.

When Ben arrived home at lunch, Mrs. Bennett was just getting Megan ready to go to the park. She was all excited to see Ben and wanted him to go to the park with them, but he told her he wanted to spend some time with Mommy. This seemed to satisfy her and she gave him a quick hug and kiss goodbye. Mrs. Bennett told Ben that Julie was in the bedroom before leaving with Megan.

Ben walked quietly to their room and found Julie sitting on the bed with her back to him looking out the window. As he walked around the bed, he could tell she was crying. He went over and sat on the bed next to her putting his arm around her. She just melted in his arms and her crying turned to uncontrollable sobs. Ben didn't know what to do or say, so he just pulled her close to him and held her, letting her cry.

She must have cried for thirty minutes before her tears started to subside. Once she seemed to be more in control, Ben told her that they needed to talk. All she did was nod. He told her that he didn't know what to say or do to help her feel better but that he wanted them to be able to talk and share and love each other the way they had before her surgery. This brought new tears to her eyes but she didn't say anything. He told her that if he had done anything to hurt her, to please tell him and they could make it right.

It was hard for Julie to talk she had cried so much and was crying again. She finally managed to ask him how he felt about losing their baby. That wasn't what he was expecting her to ask so before thinking it through, he told her that he knew that her pregnancy never could have gone to term so he had accepted that and was more worried about her making it through her surgery than anything else. He explained to her that a ruptured fallopian tube could be very dangerous and that she could have lost her life. "That's what had me terrified," he told her with tears forming in his eyes. "But what about our baby?" Julie persisted. "You never even seemed unhappy when you visited me in the hospital. Don't you even care that our baby died?"

Ben could see the hurt in her eyes and it was tearing him apart. He had no idea she felt so strongly about the loss of this child. In fact, until this moment he hadn't even considered it a loss of a child. It was too early in a pregnancy that never could have gone to term anyway. He sat there quietly for a moment and wondered what to say to her. He didn't want to hurt her more.

Finally, he took her hands in his and softly told her that of course he cared about any child of theirs'. He confessed that maybe he had been looking at it from a medical perspective and that because it had been ectopic and would have never been able to come to full term he hadn't really realized how bonded she had already become to the fetus. Julie got angry at that point and pulled away from him. "How can you call it a fetus," she screamed! "It was a baby, our baby and it died on that operating table. I don't even know if it was a boy or a girl. Nobody would tell me!"

She was crying uncontrollably again at this point. Ben didn't know whether to try and hold her again or to not touch her. She seemed so mad at him. He had never seen her like this before and it was really scaring him. "Julie, I'm so sorry," he softly said. "I didn't realize you were hurting like this. What can I do to make things better?" In between sobs, Julie told him that he could care about the loss of their child. He could hold her and grieve with her and care. All she wanted him to do was at least act like he cared, instead of being so cheerful all the time while her heart felt like it was being torn out.

Ben did hold her then, he pulled her quickly to him and with tears streaming down his face he told her that he did care. If she could only know how very much he cared. He told her that he was sorry they had lost their child and then he told her how scared he had been that he might lose her too. Not only during the surgery but for the last three weeks as she slowly slipped away from him.

As he began to sob, Julie finally responded. She put her arms around him and they sat their and cried in each other arms. This time however, it was healing tears. Ben wasn't sure how long they sat there like that but when they finally pulled apart and he kissed Julie tenderly, he saw the first hint of a smile on her face. It wasn't a big smile but it was like the sun had come out for Ben again. He hated that he had to go back to work. He would have liked to spend the whole afternoon with Julie talking and sharing and trying to better understand what she was feeling. She assured him that she would be okay now and that they would make some time that evening to talk more.

Ben washed his face and gave Julie a lingering goodbye kiss, before driving back to the office. He had a load of patients booked for that afternoon, but his heart was so much lighter as he left their house. For the first time in three weeks, he felt like things might be okay with he and Julie.

In between patients and on the way home that night, he thought about the baby that Julie had lost. He still had a hard time thinking of it as a baby, yet as he thought about Julie's reaction to him calling it a fetus, he realized more than ever how strongly she would feel about him working at the abortion clinic.

He had thought several times about telling her, but now he knew that he never would. In fact, he wondered if maybe he should quit working there at all. He never wanted to risk losing Julie. Just the last three weeks had given him an idea of how empty his life would be without her. But, then he began to think about the money he made working at the clinic and how many hours he would have to put in to make that much just seeing patients in his practice. Even though there was that nagging fear that Julie might find out, he believed that surely that would never happen since she always paged him if she needed him and she never came to the office without telling him first.

So, before he arrived home that night, he had convinced himself that they needed the extra income and there was no way Julie needed to ever know how he spent three mornings a week. Besides, he had decided to work at the clinic in the first place so they could afford a house and so he would have more time to spend with his family. Surely the end justified the means in this case. After all, he was completely within the law and these women had a right not to have a child they didn't want.

Julie actually met Ben at the door that night with a hug. Of course, Megan was right there behind her waiting for her hug. Ben couldn't even begin to express what it did to his heart to have his two favorite girls there waiting for him. It was a wonderful evening. Mrs. Bennett had fixed a delicious dinner and Julie joined in the conversation at the table. Megan was her usual talkative self and had everyone laughing.

The only sad note to the evening was at the end of the meal when Mrs. Bennett told them that she thought it was time for her to return home. Megan started to protest but Mrs. Bennett told her that she needed to go home and take care of Grandpa. He had been by himself long enough. Julie got tears in her eyes as she left her place at the table to go and give her mother a hug. They all got tearful as Julie told her how much she appreciated her being there for them and how much her love and support meant to her. "I'm just glad to see my Julie back," her mother exclaimed as she hugged her in return. Ben hated to see Mrs. Bennett go also but he knew that Julie was physically able to take care of things again and he felt for the first time that evening that she would be okay emotionally as well.

They all went to bed early that night. Ben and Julie spent some more time talking, before falling asleep. She cried some more and he comforted her and by time she feel asleep he was so exhausted he wished he could sleep for days.

As tired as he was, Ben did not sleep well that night. His old nightmare had returned but this time it was an unknown child that was begging him to help save it. Then it was Julie's face and then Megan's pleading with him to save them and help them. He tried so hard to get to them because he knew they were going to be hurt by something or someone, but he couldn't reach them in time. He woke up in the bed with a start, sweat pouring down his face.

Julie woke up as he sat up in bed and screamed "NO!" She tried to comfort him but he was shaking all over. "You must have been dreaming. What were you dreaming that upset you so much?" Julie asked. Ben tried to tell Julie about what he could remember of his dream. He didn't tell her that he'd had this dream before. He didn't want her to know that the dream started the first time he had assisted in an abortion.

He was so upset that he also failed to see how Julie was reacting to his dream. She had tears streaming down her face as she tried to comfort him. For the first time, she felt that he was grieving over the loss of their child. She thought that he had been trying so hard to be strong for her and that his grief was being expressed through this nightmare. Seeing him so vulnerable like this drew her closer to him than she had felt in a long time. They held each other close until they both fell back into a deep uninterrupted sleep.

Chapter 21

Things began to get back to normal after that night. Julie started teaching her private piano students again. She also began to enjoy and play with Megan more. The biggest change, to Ben's relief, was their relationship. If possible, they seemed to be even closer than before. They had not talked about the baby they lost much after that night that Julie had thought Ben had a nightmare about it, but he could tell her wounds were healing.

After consulting with her physician and getting a clean bill of health, they continued to try and have another child. Ben continued to work at the clinic three mornings a week and stayed busy at his practice the rest of the week. He had every weekend except one off a month, so they really enjoyed their time as a family on the weekends.

Megan was about to approach her third birthday. None of the family would be able to be present this time as Mrs. Bennett had spent so long with them after Julie's surgery, but they were going to have ten of Megan's little friends over for a birthday party. She was so excited, she could hardly wait for her birthday to come. It was hard to believe that she would be three already. It was a beautiful sunny day on her birthday. They had the party outside and everyone including the parents had a great time.

Megan was so tired that night that she fell asleep in Ben's arms as he was reading her a bedtime story. He looked down at her while she slept and felt such a rush of love for her. She was Julie made over - from her thick dark hair, to her beautiful blue eyes, to her loving and warm personality. She could melt his heart in a matter of minutes as she had done that very night when she had wrapped her arms around his neck and told him she loved him. Julie walked in as he was getting up to go put her in bed. He could tell she was tired from the days events, but she smiled and walked with him to put Megan in bed.

As they talked that night, Julie shared her concern over not being able to conceive another child yet. She told him that she didn't want Megan to grow up alone and she'd hoped that there wouldn't be such a difference in their children's ages. Ben assured her that they would keep trying and that there should be no reason why they couldn't have more children. He did remind her that her doctor told them it might take a little longer for her to conceive because she only had the one fallopian tube. "We will just have to be patient and keep trying," he reminded her with a smile as he took her in his arms to fulfill that promise.

Julie loved their house and the location but Ben continued to want to build in a new subdivision that was developing, in a higher income part of town. As Ben brought home different house plans, however, Julie joined in the excitement. In fact this seemed to help take her mind off not being able to have another child.

After several months, they found a house plan that they both liked and a lot in the new subdivision with a view of the lake. Julie wasn't sure about living that close to the lake with Megan but Ben assured her that they would fence in an area for Megan to play, so they bought the lot and the builders began to build.

They talked about putting their house on the market but just before listing it with an agent, they got a call from Julie's parents telling them that they were considering buying the house. Julie was in shock. Her father had retired earlier that year, but she never expected them to move from Chicago. Of course David would be starting college in the fall so none of the children would be left at home.

In fact David had decided to be a doctor and wanted to attend college at the University of Texas and then try to go to medical school in Houston as Ben had. They explained that since none of the other children had stayed in Chicago, they had nothing holding them there. They had saved up some money over the years and would be able to pay a big down payment, but were trying to find financing for the rest. Ben and Julie both were so surprised, but so excited. Julie had never dreamed that her parents might someday live near them.

The rest of the evening they talked about ways that they might be able to help the Bennetts find financing. In fact Ben suggested that they lower the price. Julie had wanted to ask that but she was glad it was Ben's idea. They were asking enough that they could afford to lower it for her parents. Besides, Ben had always wanted to help them have a better house anyway. He even suggested that if they couldn't find financing right away, maybe they could do a lease purchase. Julie felt so much better about leaving their house, knowing that someone she loved and that would appreciate it would be in it. She was so excited that she hardly slept that night. Her mind kept going over how great it would be to have her parents near.

The work on their house was progressing faster than they had hoped. The Bennetts had been able to find financing, especially since they had lowered the price on the house and they would be ready to move as soon as Ben and Julie were moved into their new home.

It was a busy fall for them. They all wanted to be moved in before Christmas. Ben had made a habit of going by their house every day after work to check on the progress. It seemed that the last details took the longest to get finished. It was finally finished by the end of October and Ben took a week off to get everything moved.

It was a beautiful house, with three large bedrooms and two full baths upstairs. There was also a playroom upstairs for Megan. The master bedroom suite was downstairs, with a huge bathroom with double sinks, a jacuzzi tub and a separate shower, and a walk-in closet for each of them.. There was a study for Ben, a music room for Julie, a big family room, a formal dining room and a huge eat in kitchen with a fireplace that opened to both the family room and kitchen. There was a big deck around the back of the house and a sun room off the kitchen. There were a lot of windows giving the house a bright cheerful look. In fact the family room had windows along the whole back wall.

It was so much larger than the house they moved from that their furniture looked lost in it. They had decided that their Christmas present to each other would be new family room and dining room furniture, but Julie wanted to wait until her parents were moved in so they could give them their old living room set that matched the house they had been in before.

The Bennetts were suppose to arrive the week before Thanksgiving. They had sold their house and everything was packed and ready to move. Carl had taken off some time to help them move and Julie would help them as much as she could. Ben didn't want to take any more time off because everyone was coming for Christmas and he wanted a few days then.

The move went smoothly. They got everything unpacked and organized in time to have Thanksgiving dinner at the Bennetts. Carl and David were there to celebrate with them but Carl had to go home the next day and David would go back to school on Sunday.

It seemed strange for Ben and Julie to be visiting her parents in their old house. But it also warmed Julie's heart to know her parents were there and that she could visit them whenever she wanted. It would also be nice because when everyone came for Christmas, they could stay with either the Bennetts or Ben and Julie.

Chapter 22

Christmas came before anyone was ready for it. Between Ben's patient load and moving, he and Julie had not gotten their shopping done as early as normal. They left Megan with the Bennetts the Saturday before Christmas and spent the whole day shopping. They had already purchased the new family room and dining room furniture which was their gift to each other, but they still had Megan's gifts to buy and the rest of the family to buy for. The only gift they had purchased already was for Ben's parents so that they could mail it in time for them to get it.

It was crazy at the mall so close to Christmas but Ben and Julie had fun. They hadn't been out alone in a while and they took their time and had lunch and dinner out. They were exhausted by the end of the day but were pleased with the gifts that they had purchased for everyone.

Different members of the family began to arrive within the next few days. Tommy, Ashley, Matthew and David were staying with them and Stephanie, Peter and Carl were staying at the Bennetts. They planned to have Christmas Eve dinner at the Bennetts and then all come early to open presents at Ben and Julie's. They would have their Christmas dinner later that afternoon.

Considering all the people involved everything went beautifully and the whole day was filled with noise and fun.

Megan and Matthew expecially had fun together. They were both up at the crack of dawn and seem to enjoy playing and sharing their new toys together. It amazed Ben how well everyone in the Bennett family got along. Even in all the chaos there was never any bickering or arguments. They teased each other a lot, but in a spirit of fun and love.

Their Christmas meal was wonderful. Julie and been cooking ahead before Christmas, as had Mrs. Bennett. Ben had smoked a huge turkey out in his smoker and they had so many side dishes that it was hard to get a sampling of everything on their plates. For desert they had pecan pie, lemon chess pie, Christmas cookies, and a coconut cake to choose from. It was wonderful having the whole family together around one table again. Julie was glad they had chosen a dining room table that could be expanded and that they had a large dining room. She felt that there was no better time than when a large family all sat down to have a meal together. Soon there would be more added to the table. Stephanie and Peter announced that they were expecting and Julie hoped she and Ben would be expecting again soon.

It seemed like a short visit for everyone, but they all were gone within two days after Christmas. It sure seemed quiet in their big house with only Ben, Julie and Megan. Julie could tell that her mother was sad also with the family gone. They were both glad to be near each other to cheer each other up. Ben seemed to be extremely busy after the holidays. Julie's piano students were back each week and things fell back into more of a normal routine.

Chapter 23

The next year seemed to fly by. Julie tried not to talk about it very often but was very worried that she still had not been able to conceive another child. Megan would be four years old in a few weeks and she so wanted her to have a little brother or sister. She was such a joy to their lives and when Julie really felt down she would tell herself just how thankful she should be to have Megan, and she was thankful. Megan knew how to bring sunshine to everyone around her. She had never gone through what people term "the terrible twos." Her disposition was almost always happy and cheerful. The only time she was not smiling or making others smile was when she was sick or asleep.

They planned to have a family get together on Megan's birthday, which was on a Thursday and then have a party that Saturday, at Chucky Cheese, with some of Megan's friends. Julie had rescheduled all but one of her piano lessons for that morning so that she could get the shopping done for Megan's birthday dinner that evening. She wanted to get the shopping done before 3:00 so she could bake the birthday cake while Megan napped that afternoon. They were just going to grill out hamburgers and have potato salad, corn on the cob and baked beans, so she could prepare that after Megan woke up.

Julie usually made Megan play in the house while she was giving her lessons because she liked to be able to keep an eye on her if she played outside. Even though they had a fenced area for her to play in she still felt safer if she could check on her often. However, it was such a beautiful day and before her student showed up Megan had been begging to go out and play on her gym set.

In a very grown up voice she had said, "After all Mommy, I am four years old." Julie had laughed at how grown up she tried to sound and told her that since she was four years old she could play outside, but had to stay in the fenced area. With a big smile and a skip in her step she hugged Julie and said that she would be very careful. Julie stood at the patio door as she watched Megan run to her swing. She couldn't believe how fast she was growing and how grown up she sounded sometimes. It just seemed like yesterday that they were having her first birthday and Ben's parents brought her the gym set. As she was standing there reminiscing, she heard the doorbell ring and went to let Amy, her student, into the music room.

Julie could tell that Amy hadn't practiced since the week before and the hour lesson was a very difficult one. When they finished she walked Amy to the door, reminding her to be sure and practice before next week, and then went to the patio door to get Megan, so they could go shopping.

Julie didn't see her on the swing, so she walked out to find her. She knew that Megan liked to hide so she called her as she looked through the gym set. There weren't any other places that Megan could hide in the fenced area and Julie's heart began to pound as she called out frantically for her. Her first fear was the lake so she unhooked the gate and screamed Megan's name as she ran to the edge of the water.

She had made so much noise, that several of her neighbors joined her and began to help her look for Megan. Julie didn't want to panic but she could no longer help it. Her neighbors continued to look, as she ran back to the house to call Ben and 911. She called 911 first and told them that her little girl was missing and she was afraid she might have wandered to the lake behind their house. She tried to keep the tears from coming as she talked to the lady on the other end of the line but she felt like she couldn't breath, she was so afraid.

She was so emotional by the time she called Ben, that she forgot to use his pager and called his office directly. The receptionist told her that it was his morning to work at the clinic. She could hear the panic in Julie's voice, so she quickly gave her the number there. Julie was in such a state of hysteria that she didn't even stop to wonder why Ben was at a clinic and not his office. She just mechanically dialed the number that the receptionist had given her and prayed that she would be able to get Ben quickly.

She was so frantic by the time the receptionist at the clinic answered the phone, that she practically shouted into the phone that she had to talk to Ben immediately; it was an emergency. The receptionist calmly asked her if she had an appointment and Julie lost it at that point, telling her that she didn't need an appointment. She was his wife!

It took Ben a few minutes to come to the phone but to Julie it seemed like an hour. Ben couldn't believe Julie had called him at the clinic and his first reaction was panic, that she would now know that he worked there part of the week but when he heard her voice and the near hysteria in it, his heart almost stopped. He could barely understand her but finally understood enough to realize that Megan was missing and she couldn't find her.

He told her to call the police and he would be home as fast as he could get there. He told the receptionist that there was an emergency at home and she would have to reschedule the other women for another time. He ran out the door, without any other explanation. All he could think of was Megan.

Surely she was just hiding somewhere. She loved to play hide and seek. He couldn't let himself think that she was really missing. He wouldn't have been able to drive home, if he let himself think that. As it was, he almost ran several cars off the road in his speed to get home.

As he approached their driveway, he felt this sick feeling rush over him when he saw the rescue squad truck and the police car parked in his driveway. He ran through the house and into the back yard looking for Julie. There was a large group of people gathered near the lake and he felt like his legs had turned to jelly as he tried to make his way to Julie. He wanted to call out her name but he couldn't get a sound out of his mouth. It was like one of those bad dreams when you want to call for help but your voice doesn't work.

She saw him coming and ran to meet him. She fell into his arms sobbing uncontrollably. He tried to calm her, so he could understand what had happened. Two policemen joined them and they explained as best they could that Megan had been playing in the fenced area of the backyard and when Julie had gone out to get her, she was gone.

Ben pulled Julie away from him with shaky arms, so that he could ask her some questions. He couldn't get his mind to function properly but he did ask her why Megan was outside by herself and how long she had been playing in the back yard. Julie explained through tears that she had been teaching a piano lesson and Megan had wanted to play on her gym set. She even told him how Megan had announced that she wasn't a baby anymore, that it was her birthday and she was four years old. As she recounted the conversation to Ben, she burst into a fresh bout of tears. She told Ben that it was all her fault. She should have never allowed Megan to play alone outside. Ben pulled her to him and tried to reassure her that they would find Megan and that it wasn't her fault, everything would be okay.

Ben was sure he didn't sound too reassuring because he was scared to death himself. He asked the policemen what they were doing to try and find Megan and one of them explained that they were bringing in divers to search the lake and that they were questioning the neighbors to see if they had seen anything. They needed a recent picture of Megan so that they could form several rescue groups to search the area. They explained that speed was very important because the majority of missing children who were found unharmed were found in the first few hours after they disappeared.

Somehow, Ben just couldn't make himself believe Megan was actually missing. He kept expecting her to come out of hiding any minute and dazzle them all with her infectious laugh and big dimples. Surely she was just hiding somewhere or maybe in a neighbor's kitchen enjoying some milk and cookies.

Julie had calmed down some, so he asked her to go get several pictures of Megan to give to the policemen. The divers had just arrived and Ben followed the policemen down to the lake. The rescue squad was there and they quickly organized the search of the lake. Julie ran down to the lake with several pictures. By that time, about twenty people from the neighborhood had gathered.

Julie had called her mother and father and they drove up, just as several search groups were being formed. Ben was going to lead one search group and Mr. Bennett volunteered to lead another. They had a policeman, several rescue personnel and five or six neighbors in each group. Scott, a tall athletic looking man who appeared to be in charge of the rescue team, explained which areas each team would search. They were to cover the neighborhood within a two mile radius. They were to knock on doors and ask if anyone had seen Megan or anyone in the neighborhood who seemed suspicious or had never been seen before. He told them to get all the details they could and to look in every place that she might be hiding.

Julie wanted to go with one of the groups, but Scott explained to her that she needed to stay at home in case Megan came back. Mrs. Bennett could see that Julie was an emotional wreck so she told Ben that she would stay with her. Julie decided to go back to the lake and watch the divers. One part of her was afraid to be there, in case they found Megan's body but another part of her couldn't stay away. She had to know, whatever they found. Besides, she couldn't stand being in the house, not knowing what was happening. Her mother had thought they should wait in the house but Julie needed to be doing something.

They stood by the lake for about an hour watching the divers as they meticulously searched the lake. Each time they would surface, Julie thought her heart would pound out of her chest. She was so afraid Megan might have fallen in the lake and drowned even though they had warned her time and time again to never go near the water. But each time they came up empty handed, she felt this surge of relief that made her knees feel like they might buckle.

Finally, she felt so weak that she had to sit down on the grass. Mrs. Bennett sat beside her and put her arm around her. That was all Julie needed to bring on the tears again. She thought she had cried so much already that there could be no tears left. Her mom just held her and let her cry.

After her tears had subsided, she confided to her mother that she should have never let Megan play outside by herself when she couldn't check on her for a whole hour. Julie was feeling so guilty, blaming herself for Megan's disappearance. She was so afraid of what might have happened to her. "Mom, I just can't believe she would leave the fenced area and go near the lake," Julie reasoned. "We had talked to her so many times about that. But, if she didn't come down here, then where is she? Could she just be hiding somewhere?" Julie asked hopefully.

Then her face clouded over and panic set in again. "Oh Mom, what if someone took her. She's always so friendly to everyone, what if someone came up to the fence and took her?" Julie said, with a look of sheer terror on her face. Mrs. Bennett tried to comfort Julie by telling her not to create all these horrible scenarios in her mind. "We have to believe one of the search groups will find her," she said. "I don't believe she fell in the lake. I believe that any minute someone will be bringing her back to us."

They sat their for another hour, while the divers finished searching the lake, finding nothing. Julie was so relieved and a ray of hope began to form itself in her heart. She was sure Ben would come back with Megan. If anyone could find her Ben would. He would never give up without finding Megan, she reassured herself.

Julie's mother had gone back to the house to make some coffee and sandwiches for the divers and rescue group that had searched the lake. It was hard for Julie to make herself go back into the house without Megan, but she tried to busy herself helping her mom. Just as the divers finished eating, Julie heard her father's voice. She ran to the front yard, fully expecting them to have Megan with them. Her heart sank when she saw the dejected look on her dad's face. "We looked everywhere, Julie," Mr Bennett said. "We didn't see her or find anyone who had any information."

"Oh dad," Julie cried. "I don't think I can stand this. We have to find her before dark. She's afraid of the dark and she's so little and defenseless!" Her father pulled her too him and tried to reassure her that he was sure the other group would find her. She tried not to feel totally despondent and to hold on to the hope that Ben would find Megan.

Some of the neighbors, who had helped her father's group search, decided to go back to their homes. They hugged Julie and told her that they were available to help in any way that they could. Julie and her father went back into the house to get the rescue workers from his group something to eat and drink. As Julie was putting ice into paper cups for them she spotted the cake mix on the counter for Megan's cake. This made her break down again. Her mother ran over to her and took her into the den. She told her to lie down for a while and she and Mr. Bennett would take care of the rescue workers.

Julie sat on the couch but she couldn't bring herself to lie down. Too many scary thoughts kept entering her mind. Where was Ben and his group and why was it taking them so long? What had they found? She was just getting up from the couch, because she couldn't stand this immobility any longer, when she heard Ben outside. She, her mom and dad just about ran into each other in their haste to get to Ben. She thought she might die when she saw the look on his face and saw that Megan was not with him.

Ben led her back to the couch and Scott and the two policemen followed them back into the den. Mr. And Mrs. Bennett stood in the doorway, waiting to hear what Ben seemed to be trying to say. He took Julie's hands in his and started several times to say something but the words just wouldn't come out. He was trying so hard to stay in control but the tears were flowing and this was scaring Julie to death.

Finally, Scott told them that they hadn't found any sign of Megan but that one of the neighbors they had questioned thought she saw her looking out the window of a van, as it drove out of the neighborhood. They were able to describe the van and said that the driver was a middle aged man, with blond hair and a mustache. One of the policeman had immediately phoned in an APB and they had contacted the FBI.

Julie felt like all the blood had drained from her. She turned so white and took so long to respond that Ben was worried that she was about to pass out. Her worst fears were a reality.

How could someone have taken Megan from their back yard without her hearing a thing. She barely heard the policemen ask Ben a series of questions. She finally tuned back in as they asked if he knew of anyone or any reason that someone might want to kidnap Megan. Ben couldn't think of any reason why anyone would want to take his little girl much less harm her in any way. He couldn't let himself think of that. It made him so angry inside and yet he felt so helpless.

Scott asked him about their financial status and if someone might have taken Megan for a ransom. Ben told him that they had a modest savings but were not wealthy by any means. However, his parents were very wealthy. What if someone that knew his parents had kidnapped Megan to get money from them? He realized then that he hadn't even contacted his parents. The police suggested that he call them and fill them in on what they knew at this point, in case they were called by the kidnapper.

Ben didn't really want to call his parents and if someone had taken his Megan because of his parent's wealth, he didn't know if he could ever forgive that. He knew in his heart it wasn't his parents fault but at this moment he couldn't think reasonably about anything. He just wanted Megan back, unharmed.

Julie still had not said a word as Ben got up to call his parents. She sat there, as if she were in a trance. Her father and mother came over and sat on either side of her. They too were worried about her. Her dad put his arm around her and she finally responded by melting into his arms and crying great, racking sobs. The policemen and Scott left the room and went into the kitchen so they could be alone for a few minutes. They knew how hectic things were going to get as soon as the FBI arrived, sat up their equipment and started asking all their questions.

Much to Ben's surprise, he was able to reach his parents at home. They were devastated and wanted to fly to Houston immediately, but Ben explained that they needed to stay by their phone, in case Megan had been kidnapped by someone wanting a ransom from them. His father couldn't imagine that would happen but he agreed to let Ben know immediately if someone called. His mother was in tears and asked him to keep them informed as soon as they knew anything at all. He actually felt his heart melt a little toward his parents at their genuine concern. He promised to let them know as soon as they heard anything and his father actually said "We love you," before hanging up the phone.

Ben went back into the den to find Julie sobbing as her father held her. He instantly thought of the times Megan had crawled up in his lap and cried about a hurt knee or about a little bug or something that had been hurt. His chest felt like someone had taken a rope and was squeezing it so tight, he could hardly breathe. He remembered the times he had held Megan and promised her he would never let anyone hurt her. He had failed miserably in this promise. He felt like he had to do something or he might go crazy.

He wanted to go hold Julie and comfort her but he couldn't. He turned around without saying a word and left the house. He went down to the lake and walked around hoping that the lady who told them about seeing Megan in the van had been mistaken. Hoping that at any minute Megan would come out of hiding and tell them it had all been a game and she had been hiding from them. Surely no one would hurt her. How could anyone hurt a beautiful little girl like Megan? He sat on the bank of the lake and cried like he had never cried before. They had to find her. He couldn't stand not knowing where she was or what was happening to her. She must be so afraid and he couldn't help her.

Finally, when he felt that there were no more tears left, he just sat there staring at the water, trying not to think at all. He felt, more than saw Julie come and sit down beside him, putting her arm through his. In a way, he wanted to blame her for not watching Megan closely enough but he knew that wasn't fair. He knew Julie loved Megan as much as he did. He slipped his arm around her and they sat there silently, grieving together.

Finally, he told her that they both needed to be strong for Megan's sake and that they needed to believe that no matter what, she would be found unharmed and brought back to them. "We have to believe that, Julie," he said. She seemed to draw strength from him and agreed that they would not think of the bad things that could happen to Megan but believe that they would have her back again soon. Just as they were about to get up and return to the house, her mother called to them from the back door, telling them that the FBI had arrived.

The FBI set up their equipment in Ben's study. They were not nearly as friendly and comforting as the local police. In fact for the first few hours they pounded Ben and Julie with questions. First they questioned them together and then separately. Ben was beginning to get very angry as it seemed they were more concerned with questioning them instead of trying to find Megan.

They finally seemed to be satisfied that it was some type of abduction and that there had been no fowl play on the part of Ben or Julie. Ben was almost ready to order them from his house for even giving a hint of suggesting that he or Julie might have harmed Megan. Mr. Bennett stepped in and took him aside. He told him that it was just probably routine questioning and that they needed the police and FBI in order to hopefully get Megan back. Ben calmed down then and asked where Julie had gone.

He found her in Megan's room, sitting on her bed holding Megan's favorite stuffed bear. She was rocking it back and forth and tears were streaming down her face. He went to her and sat beside her putting his arm around her. For a while they didn't talk and then Julie said, "Ben, she must be so afraid. I can't stand the thought of her being out there without us frightened and alone.." "I can't stand it and yet there is nothing I can do about it. I don't feel as if I can bare this!" "I know," Ben said as he pulled her closer to him." "I feel so helpless too. All Megan's life I promised her I would protect her and never let anything harm her. Now, I've failed her and she is out there, who knows where, with some psycho." This thought brought a new rush of tears to Julie's eyes. "No!" she shouted as she pulled away from him. "I won't believe someone could harm her. I won't think about that and I won't believe it." She rushed from the room and Ben just sat there and cried.

Chapter 24

The next 48 hours were a big blur. Julie slept off and on; an hour nap here and there, but Ben hardly slept at all and when he did lie down and try to sleep, he kept having his recurring nightmare. However, this time it was Megan that kept calling to him for help and he couldn't get to her to help her. He would wake up in a sweat, with his heart pounding in his chest. After he had dreamed this twice, he tried not to sleep anymore.

Julie's parents were staying with them around the clock and her brothers and sisters had called many times. Ben's parents called every few hours but they had received no ransom calls. As the hours ticked by Ben and Julie both began to fear the worst. They couldn't bear the thought of Megan being with some stranger, afraid and not knowing where they were and why they didn't come and get her. More than that, they couldn't stand to think that he might hurt her in any way. They had never really gone to church or had a belief in God, but they would lift up a prayer when their hearts were about to break, that Megan would not be hurt. They didn't even realize who they were praying to, but they felt so powerless that they didn't know what else to do.

The FBI had pictures of Megan printed and they spent some of their time distributing and posting them throughout town. They were on the local news showing a picture of

Megan and asking for any information that anyone might have. They also gave a discription of the van and the man seen driving it, in hopes that someone would have seen it and report it to the police or FBI.

With each passing day, hope seemed a little harder to find. There were so many reminders of Megan everywhere they looked. Julie would spend hours sitting in Megan's room holding one of her favorite stuffed animals and crying. The hardest thing was not knowing what had happened to her or what she might be going through. They wanted news so badly but they were afraid everytime the telephone rang.

They received many calls each day with someone saying they thought they had seen her. The FBI followed up on every lead but came up empty handed. Ben hadn't seen any of his patients in a week. Neither of them had hardly eaten or slept in a week. Everytime Ben tried to sleep he would start to have the nightmare and so he tried to sleep as little as he possible. He tried to be as comforting to Julie as he could be but he had to constantly fight wanting to place the blame on someone. Half the time, he found himself blaming her and the rest of the time, he blamed himself for not being able to protect Megan.

He wanted to feel close to Julie. He needed to feel that and he knew that she needed him but it was like he was operating in a vacumn and if he let his feelings go or talked about them, he might lose control completely or he might lose all hope. The feeling he remembered most was helplessness and emptiness.

Julie had finally laid down out of sheer exhaustion and had been sleeping for about five hours when the FBI received a call from the police in a town on the outskirts of Dallas saying they had found a body that might be Megan and wanted someone to come and try to identify it. Ben felt as if his heart had stopped when the agent told him about the call. He knew he had to go look at the body but he didn't know if he could do it.

He woke Julie and told her as gently as he could that they had found a little girl's body but didn't know if it was Megan and that he was leaving in an hour to go identify it. Ben felt that it would be better for Julie to stay at home and he would go alone but she immediately said that she wanted to be there with him. As they were getting ready to go, Mrs Bennett was preparing them some sandwiches and coffee. She was so worried about Julie. She shared with her husband that she was worried that Julie would go back into the deep depression that she had been in, when she lost the baby over a year ago.

When Ben and Julie came into the kitchen to get the coffee and sandwiches, Mr. Bennett came over and put his arm around Julie and asked her wouldn't she rather he go with Ben and she stay home with her mother? Actually, Julie couldn't decide whether she wanted to go or not. She was so tired of being in this house waiting and wanted so much to know what had happened to Megan, but she didn't want this to be her. The only thing that was keeping her sane, was the hope that they would find Megan alive. So one part of her wanted to go and another wanted to stay there and keep hoping, as long as possible.

The FBI was flying them, by helicopter, to Dallas and wanted to leave as soon as possible so Ben went to Julie and took her in his arms. He had been watching her struggle with whether to go or not and it wasn't the first time since this all happened, that he felt a deep concern and love for her wash over him. He didn't know what he would find in Dallas and he didn't know how he would handle it if this little girl was Megan, but he did know that he loved Julie with all his heart and wanted to protect her from what they might find.

For days he had felt so powerless in his ability to protect Megan but at least he could protect Julie from this. He gently told her that he thought it would be best if she stayed and let her father go with him. He promised to come home as soon as he identified the body and let her know if it was Megan. He also told her for the first time since this had happened how much he loved her. Julie needed to hear that so desperately, because she blamed herself and worried daily that Ben didn't love her anymore because he blamed her also.

As he held her, she felt his warmth and strength and she began to feel stronger. She knew that they could face whatever happened as long as they could talk and continue to love each other. She agreed to stay and let her father go if that's what he thought was best. Ben kissed her gently before pulling away from her to tell the FBI agent that they were ready.

The flight seemed to last forever to Ben. In one way, Ben wanted to hurry and get there and in another he dreaded it with every fiber of his being. On the way, the FBI agent explained that they would first go to the police station and then to the county morgue to identify the body.

The police were very accommodating and friendly. He could tell that there was more to the story than he had heard thus far because they all looked at him with such pity. Detective Morris led them into his office and offered them coffee. He seemed to be prolonging talking to them as long as he could. Finally, he told them that this was one of the most difficult cases he'd had since becoming a detective.

Ben sat frozen in his chair, as Detective Morris told him that he wanted to prepare him, before he went to the morgue, for what he would see. He told Ben that the little girl they had found was terribly mutilated and burned. Ben thought he might pass out as he explained how and where they had found the body. At this point, they had no suspects. They had received a call the night before from a group of teenagers who had been hiking in a wooded area nearby and had discovered the body. It appeared as if the body had been there for only a few days, but some of the body parts were missing. Ben didn't know if he could endure hearing any more. He looked at his father-in-law and saw that he too looked as if he might pass out at any moment.

The ride to the morgue seemed to end too quickly. Ben wasn't sure if he could do this. Mr. Bennett offered to go in with him to see the body but Ben told him that he would really rather do it alone. One of the detectives and the coroner went into the room with him. The room was cool, damp and depressing. The coroner went to one of the refrigerated compartments and opened the door. Ben slowly walked over to the table that was pulled out.

They let him take his time in removing the sheet covering the body. Ben had tried to prepare himself on the drive over and had told himself over and over that this wouldn't be his Megan. He took a deep breath, held it and slowly pulled back the sheet.

What he saw was something he could have never prepared himself for. His beautiful little girl lay there cold and lifeless. Part of her face had burns on it marring her beauty and innocence but she was clearly recognizable. He pulled back the rest of the sheet before the detective could stop him and saw what this monster had done to his daughter before the room turned black and he passed out. Before he passed out however, he had instant flashes of some of the burned and mutilated babies that he had helped to abort.

When he had came to, he was on a couch in the coroner's office and at first, he didn't know where he was. He saw his father-in-law sitting in a chair, across the room, with his head buried in his hands sobbing and then the horrible reality came back to him. He wished he could have passed out again, because the pain that he felt at that moment was unbearable. The detective offered to get them a room for the night but all Ben wanted was to leave this place and never come back. He couldn't even talk to the detective or coroner. Mr. Bennett had to make all the arrangements to have the body flown home.

187

As they flew back home, Ben couldn't even let himself think. He had to keep the horrible picture of Megan out of his mind. He couldn't bear thinking of it yet. The memory of seeing her was too fresh. He had no idea how he would tell Julie. He couldn't tell her what had been done to Megan. How could anyone do this kind of thing to a defenseless little child? Then he remembered the flashes of those small aborted babies that he'd had before passing out. Had he been doing something just as bad to small defenseless little babies? His mind was not able to continue this line of thought. He would block it out for now and not think about it. He was in no way like this monster who had murdered his Megan.

There was complete silence in the helicopter as they flew back. The FBI agent told him that they would be in touch with him in a few days and promised him that they would do all within their power to catch the person who had done this.

Chapter 25

That was four days ago and now here he was sitting at Megan's funeral. He had completely lost track of what the minister was saying, but it didn't matter. All that mattered was that he and Julie would never see Megan again. In fact, Julie had not seen her body when they flew it back and they had a closed casket ceremony. He was the only one that had seen her and would have to carry the memory of her mutilated body with him for the rest of his life.

It had been a sleepless few days since he returned and he was drained and tired. He squeezed Julie's hand as the minister finished his prayer and then they exited the church to go to the cemetery. This would be the hardest part for him. He couldn't imagine his little girl being lowered into the ground and covered by dirt forever. As he watched this whole process, it was like he was another person watching, some automatic person who moved and spoke but didn't feel anything. That was the only way he knew to get through this, to shut off all his feelings, until her funeral was over and he could be alone with them. For now he had to be strong for Julie. They had both cried so much the last few weeks. He didn't seem to have any tears left. All he felt now was a painful emptiness, guilt, and anger.

The rest of that day seemed to go by in a blur. He remembered riding home and Mrs. Bennett trying to get them to eat something for dinner. He remembered his mother and father and all of Julie's family being there at the house but he just walked around in this foggy state. He wanted so much to go into his quiet bedroom and lie down on the bed and sleep for a very long time. If he could just get away from all these people and sleep. Then he wouldn't have to think of anything, just sleep.

However, it was past eleven o'clock that night when he and Julie finally got to bed. They had hardly spoken since the funeral and they weren't sure what to say to each other now. Julie was crying as she got into bed and he pulled her close to him, without saying a word, and held her until he felt her body relax in sleep. It wasn't until then, that he could let himself fall asleep.

The dream Ben dreamed that night would change his life forever. It seemed as if he had just fallen asleep when the dream began. It was such a clear dream. He wasn't even in the dream, he was just an observer. It was Megan's birthday in the dream and she was playing outside alone. First she played on her gym set and then got in her swing. She was talking to a make believe friend, when a van drove up and a man came over to the fence. Ben could hear him say "Hey, little girl, I have a treat for you, come over here." He saw Megan trying to decide whether to talk to him or not, then she shyly asked, "Is it a birthday present?" The man got a sly smile on his face and said, "Sure I've got a special birthday present for you in my van. Come over here with me and we'll get it." Megan only hesitated a minute before leaving the swing to walk toward the fence. Ben wanted to yell for her to stop and not go near the man but he wasn't a part of the dream; he could only observe. Just as Megan was about to approach the fence, a little girl who looked to be about seven or eight walked down the side walk toward their house. "Hi, Angela." he heard Megan say. "Do you want to come with me to see my new birthday present?" As Angela drew nearer, the man panicked and ran back to his van and sped away. Angela came into the fenced area to play with Megan. This Angela, whom Ben had never seen before had just saved his little girl's life. Ben was so happy he wanted to shout for joy. Megan wasn't really dead she had been saved. But wait, had he really never seen Angela before. All of a sudden this wonderful, marvelous dream that Ben wanted so much to be true, turned into a nightmare beyond compare. He knew without a shadow of a doubt who Angela was. She was that first little baby girl that he had aborted. The one that he had dreamed about all these years. All of a sudden Angela and Megan and all these little babies began to reach out to him and cry out in pain. They were being burned and torn apart. They were crying "Help me, save me. Why are you hurting me?" The tortuous looks on their faces were unbearable. Just as he thought he might die from the helplessness and pain he felt for these children, he woke up and sat straight up in bed. Sweat was dripping from his face and neck. His heart was beating so fast that he thought it might pound out of his chest. He knew that it had been a dream but he also began to realize, with this sick feeling of reality that if he had never aborted that first little girl, his Megan would be asleep right now in the safey of her bed. Instead she was under that cold hard ground, torn and mutilated, like all the other little babies that had been senselessly destroyed.

But, what would never be known was the incredible difference that could have been made by the lives of these discarded children.

Psalms 139: 13 - 16

"For you have formed my inward parts;
You have covered me in my mother's womb.
I will praise You for I am fearfully and
wonderfully made.
Marvelous are Your works, and that
my soul knows very well.
My frame was not hidden from You
when I was made in secret, and
skillfully wrought in the lowest
parts of the earth.
Your eyes saw my substance, being
yet unformed.
And in Your book, they all were written,
the days fashioned for me,
When as yet there were none of them.
How precious also are your thoughts
to me, O Lord, how great is the sum
of them."

NOTE FROM THE AUTHOR

I hope you have found this book thought provoking. I have had several comments from readers that the ending has a sad and unfinished feeling. That was purposeful because abortion leaves many lives sad and unfinished. As a Director of two different crisis pregnancy centers, I saw the devastating effects of abortion on women, men, and families. I believe because our society today can discard lives so easily, we have indeed "lost our innocence" as a society and a Nation. However, I, as well as my fellow Christian readers, know that God can take even the most devastating situations and turn them around for His glory and purposes.

My plan is to demonstrate this in my next book "Redeemed Lives". This book will focus on God's forgiveness, healing and redemption. God will continue to use this little aborted girl, Angela, to touch Ben's life, eventually leading him to the only source of forgiveness, peace and redemption, our Lord and Savior, Jesus Christ.

My prayer is that you will be able to use "Discarded Lives" as an instrument for working God's will in the lives of others; that you will share it with someone you know that may be pro-choice or not sure how they feel about abortion. I believe that they will read "Discarded Lives", as my pro-life beliefs are not fully disclosed until the end of the book. This also was purposeful because some people can convince themselves that abortion is a free choice, legal and therefore okay. Those of us who are pro-life know that it is really a loss of life, great human potential, and innocence. It affects each and every one of us. As we see in Psalm 139, God has a plan and purpose for every precious life, even as he or she is being formed in their mother's womb. HE knows because HE is God and we are not.